You've Got This!

D0111240

You've Got This!

The 5 Self-Coaching Keys
You Need to Live Boldly
and Accomplish Anything

WILL MATTHEWS

New York

You've Got This!
The 5 Self-Coaching Keys You Need to Live Boldly and Accomplish Anything

© 2017 WILL MATTHEWS

Published in New York, New York, by Morgan James Publishing. Morgan James and The Entrepreneurial Publisher are trademarks of Morgan James, LLC. www.MorganJamesPublishing.com

The Morgan James Speakers Group can bring authors to your live event. For more information or to book an event visit The Morgan James Speakers Group at www.TheMorganJamesSpeakersGroup.com.

Shelfie

A **free** eBook edition is available with the purchase of this print book.

CLEARLY PRINT YOUR NAME ABOVE IN UPPER CASE

Instructions to claim your free eBook edition:
1. Download the Shelfie app for Android or iOS
2. Write your name in **UPPER CASE** above
3. Use the Shelfie app to submit a photo
4. Download your eBook to any device

ISBN 978-1-68350-052-0 paperback
ISBN 978-1-68350-053-7 eBook
ISBN 978-1-68350-054-4 hardcover
Library of Congress Control Number:
2016906532

Cover Design by:
Rachel Lopez
www.r2cdesign.com

Interior Design by:
Bonnie Bushman
The Whole Caboodle Graphic Design

with...

In an effort to support local communities, raise awareness and funds, Morgan James Publishing donates a percentage of all book sales for the life of each book to

Habitat for Humanity Peninsula and Greater Williamsburg.
Get involved today! Visit
www.MorganJamesBuilds.com

Table of Contents

Acknowledgments

When I interviewed Mark Victor Hansen, co-author of the publishing phenomenon, *Chicken Soup for the Soul* book series, on my radio program, he said something that I will never forget. Mark told me that he never entered into any project, venture or business on his own. He always had at least one partner. That is how I approached the writing of this book. This book would not be half of what it is without the amazing contributions of the following people.

Nancy Hutchins for her grounding and effective editing and counsel. I had worked with four other editors before finding Nancy and I am deeply appreciative for her guidance, professionalism and commitment to making sure that the passages that make up this book held true to my voice.

Thanks to Kelly Johnson, my assistant and go to person for all of the administrative things that it takes to run my business and especially for helping keep this book project moving forward.

The many people who read and reread the manuscript and offered feedback and ideas that dramatically improved the readability and presentation of the book, especially John Matthews and Mandy Reisman. Thank you both so much for always being willing to read through a chapter "just one more time."

To the clients that I have had the honor of working with over these past years, many of whose stories are included in this book, for their openness, perseverance, commitment to excellence and willingness to explore and expand. It has been amazing to watch and participate as you have shifted from doubt to strength, shown the power of the human spirit and become Warriors, taking the reins and creating your destinies.

Thank you all.

Live Life Full Out

"Far better is it to dare mighty things, to win glorious triumphs, even though checkered by failure... than to rank with those poor spirits who neither enjoy nor suffer much, because they live in a gray twilight that knows not victory nor defeat."
—Theodore Roosevelt

R ight now, and in every second of every day, you have important choices that only *you* can make. You can play small or live large. You can settle or you can jump in with both feet. You can shrink back... or you can be a Warrior—brave, bold and courageous.

This book is, in large measure, a call to action, a call to become more—to really go for it and to live an outstanding life—to let go of all the BS, to be grateful for everything that's already working in your life, and to commit to being resilient. To answer the call means you'll be willing to go back to the drawing board from time to time, dump the old script and write a new one. During this process, you'll connect or, perhaps reconnect, to the understanding that you are connected, protected, guided and loved and that all that's really needed is to trust that the universe is, indeed, a friendly and safe place for you to experiment, explore your capabilities and grow. In addition, you will learn to be wise and strong enough to let go of that which no longer serves you.

The most exciting thing is that whatever choices you make, this universal energy that moves in and through each of us and connects us to each other and all things is compelled to support you. If you choose to live your life playing small, only small opportunities will show up for you. The great news is that (*listen closely now*) if you decide to go for it, to reach for your dreams, you will be supported. The universal connecting energy is only waiting for you to commit, and it will bring you big opportunities, phenomenal contacts at just the right time, and knowledge in the form of insight and intuition that will keep you moving toward the fulfillment of your dreams.

I know what you may be thinking... I can't dream big... but yes, you can... and this book will show you how people are doing it. Will there be tough times and challenges that will show up when you play at a higher level? Of course there will be. That is just part of the process and will test your mettle.

This book is in your hands right now to give you the tools you need to stand strong on your journey, to master your emotions, your state of mind, your energy, your time—and most importantly, your future.

Not long ago, I was on a subway in New York where I overheard a conversation that I seem to hear a lot. A man and woman, both appearing to be in their mid-thirties, were expressing their frustrations with their career choices and how trapped they felt. I was amazed at their intensity as they detailed exactly what they hated about their jobs—the people they worked for, the commute into Manhattan, the mismatch of their daily tasks to their skills. What were they doing spending ten hours a day in something that was driving them that crazy? The doors opened and they both left the train, undoubtedly feeling that what they had to look forward to was ten thousand more days of this same soul-crushing experience.

By the way, if you hate *your* job, like the two people on the subway, you are not alone. According to Gallop's 2013 "State of the American Workplace Report" in which 150,000 workers were polled, just 30% said they were engaged and inspired by their jobs. *30%???* When asked how they ended up in the occupation they had, many stated that it was "just the best deal I could find at the time." WOW, the best deal that they could find at the time? Not exactly taking the reins. There is another way, though—a way that stems from a commitment to be deliberate and drive your own destiny. It involves thoughtful, committed change—the result of which is nothing short of amazing, transforming, and empowering.

This book was created to provide an easy-to-read, easy-to-use road map for mastering mental, emotional, physical, spiritual and interpersonal ways of approaching your life. This is about living *full* out and not being *left* out. We are left out when we stand on the sidelines and never step into the game because we are fearful. Human beings and computers operate in similar ways. Left unprotected, computers can become contaminated by malicious viruses that kill productivity and cause tremendous stress for their owners. These viruses transform a machine that's engineered to run flawlessly and with clear purpose into a nightmare of lost productivity, frustration and disappointment.

Like computers, we come from the "factory" equipped to operate on purpose, effectively and successfully. As we grow and take on more and more information, we allow small but powerful changes to our operating system that affect our ability to perform at our best—or in some cases, to perform at all. We allow in and adopt a myriad of new "rules" in the form of beliefs about ourselves, our abilities, our value, our shortcomings, our good or bad fortune, our lot in life, what is possible for us… our destiny.

You've Got This! is an invitation to scan your hard drive and to take a good look at the rules you may have unknowingly embraced or at those that were installed by someone else in your life, or even society in general, all without your knowing it. This is especially true for the rules that are standing like walls between you and what you most want… and what you most want to experience. We are constantly building a case in support of our own set of rules. When we are faced with decisions, our rules dictate which path we choose. For the couple that I saw on the subway, their rules had actually derailed them from a path of passion, growth and authenticity and, instead, landed them in a place where they settled for "the best deal I could find at the time." It is critical to know that a disempowering rule left unchallenged becomes a personal limit—a limit to growth, to contribution, to development, to satisfaction.

In the pages that follow, you will have the opportunity to explore five essential disciplines that, once understood and implemented, will not only guide you toward your own knowing that, no matter what you choose to achieve, *you've got this!*, but will also help you stay committed, resourceful and focused so that you will contribute and succeed full out. You will learn how to implement the 5 self-coaching keys you need to live boldly and accomplish anything.

During my career in professional development, I have been fortunate to witness profound life-changes. Let me give you an example of one of those. When Raj, a 45-year-old housewife, mother of two, and manager of the family business, came to me for coaching and guidance, she was at her wit's end. She had allowed herself to be relegated to doing *everything* for everyone in her family—including all the cooking and cleaning, looking after the children, taking care of her aging parents, AND taking primary responsibility for the family business. Everyone else in the family seemed to have an excuse as to why they couldn't pitch in and, frankly, did very little to help in any of these areas. She lived every day in overwhelm, resentment and stress. Understandably, she was afraid that her life was going to go by without her having any time or energy to pursue her own dreams. And she was also afraid that if she pushed back or said "no," she would not be loved… and perhaps even rejected.

Through our work together, Raj found new strength and clarity, and today she is a new woman. She has, in fact, chased and captured her dream and is a successful Marketing Team Lead in a thriving marketing firm. While that alone is so great, even more beautiful is the fact that, instead of being rejected for saying "no" to what was clearly an unfair set of expectations, she is respected and admired even more by her parents, husband and children. Raj finally *got it!*

What are you saying "Yes" to that you now need to say "No" to?

Greg is another example. When we met, he was a 35-year-old financial advisor who had achieved exceptional success in his field, but he had begun to feel that each sales call was painful because it felt so pushy and required him to be someone that he, frankly, didn't like very much. Finally, in the middle of one of his meetings with a prospective client, a meeting that seemed to be going nowhere, Greg stopped the conversation and said, "You know what, I feel like I am trying to talk you into something, and I don't want to feel that way. If it's okay with you, let's just start over human-to-human, not salesperson-to-prospect. What, if anything, are you interested in hearing about the financial services that we offer?"

The two rebooted their conversation and went on to talk about the prospect's concerns regarding his family's financial security. It had seemed like just another sales call. But for Greg, it was the beginning of a complete transformation—a whole new way of approaching his business. Almost spontaneously, he found himself listening with a completely new purpose. Having experienced how incredibly good it felt to drop the facade and simply show up authentically as himself, Greg made that his way of being in every meeting… and subsequently found his sales meetings to be fun and much more satisfying. As a result, he became massively successful and became a top producer in his office. Greg finally *got it!* He identified self-imposed, stale rules, made changes, and installed new, powerful rules that worked for him.

Susan was crushin' it in her job as a sales manager for a telecommunications company. Quarter in and quarter out, her sales numbers always ranked within the top two out of the forty-three sales teams around the country. Her bonuses were significant, and her career was allowing her to create a desirable lifestyle for herself and her family. Everything was going exceedingly well. Or was it? Susan discovered that financial success, as highly valued as it is by most people, does not translate directly into personal happiness. Instead, Susan felt a painful emptiness, and as much as she alternated between renouncing it and rationalizing it, there was no denying that the emptiness was there and growing. She came to me looking for ideas and strategies for determining if she should stay in her current role or make a change. Six months later, she made the transition from her corporate gig to a leadership-consulting career. For Susan, this was the moment in which she finally committed. *You've got this!* finally meant something to her on a visceral level, and ever since then, she's never looked back.

Every change in our external circumstances begins with a powerful internal shift. The change in Raj's circumstances began with a single decision to reclaim her future. The life-changing shift for Greg was born in a moment when he realized that he could be authentic and real—and still be exceptionally successful. For Susan, the change came in a single moment of recognition that she had *options* and that it was entirely up to her—stay on the path she was on or pick another. These were defining moments.

Change. Yeah, it can be tough to initiate. It can seem risky. That is why so many of us shy away from making important changes. But guess what, risk is the precursor to freedom, expansion and an authentic and rewarding life. No doubt about it—risk includes challenges, and challenges are often the most powerful of all gifts. It is your challenges that force you to discover who you really are—and open the door to becoming the person you really want to be. If your life is bland and unexciting, it is time to make a change. You are the only one that can determine if you will live full out or be left out.

Big challenges often come early in life. A young boy is contemplating asking a girl to dance for the first time in his life. In that moment, he feels that everything is on the line, that his whole future hinges on her response. If she says "yes," then everything will be awesome. But what if she says "no" or laughs at him… and everyone in the room sees it? That would be terrifying. That would be failure. That would be the worst thing ever. His decision to move forward, to go ahead and ask her instead of shrinking back and taking the safe road is a defining moment.

A senior manager with a multi-national manufacturing company feels a tug in his heart that he wants to spend his time and energy completely differently than he has so far. He wants to start his own business and help other people in a way that is more focused and personal than he can be in his executive role. His decision to embrace the risk and step boldly into the unknown—or to shrink back into the safety of the corporate security blanket became a defining moment.

We can wait and hope for defining moments to show up and motivate us to grow, stretch and succeed, or we can choose to embrace the fact that having what we want is, quite simply, a choice. Your choices right now define your future.

- Being unstoppable is a choice.
- Being resilient is a choice.
- Having what you want is a choice.
- Settling and giving in is a choice.
- Getting back up, dusting yourself off, and getting back into the race is a choice.
- Buying into excuses is a choice.
- Being courageous is a choice.
- Digging in and dominating or letting opportunities slip away is a choice.

Let's step it up, starting right now… and really live this life that we have been given. We all have the option to give up, to give in. But if you picked up this book, you are not that person.

Left unchecked, you will accumulate and take ownership of some amazingly damaging thoughts, beliefs and rules about yourself and your place in the world. You have the ability and, in my opinion, the responsibility to be ready to reinvent yourself in any moment. It is this ability that is the greatest gift and greatest asset that you have, for this is your "Get out of Jail Free" card—and it never expires.

Your inherent ability to reinvent yourself means that you can open any door no matter how strong the lock and can shatter any bars that are holding you back. This "jail" is different for each of us. For some, the jail that we live in is a painful relationship. For others, jail is a stale and unrewarding job. For still others, jail is addiction or poor physical fitness, low energy, and a lethargic approach to life.

Come on. Trust yourself, stretch yourself. Use your "Get out of Jail Free Card" right now and start playing a bigger game. I'll show you how. Find out for yourself what your limits really are.

If you have ever really watched a baby, you can learn a ton about life. For a baby, everything is interesting, and there is no concept of "impossible." This is still who you are at your core. Is it finally time now to let go of all your self-imagined limitations? Yes, let go! Happiness and massive growth are often just on the other side of releasing and letting go of anything that no longer serves or supports you.

Yours can be a legacy of passion and enthusiasm. Don't be the kind of person that takes the easiest of roads, the road of mediocrity, the road of playing small. That road, by the way, is the road that claims the highest toll… *on your soul.*

Right now, in this moment, begin to challenge and let go of any thought that holds you to the status quo, to old tired versions of what is possible. Everything great that has ever taken place was the result of someone letting go of what was held as normal or acceptable. Galileo took his very life in his hands when he proclaimed that the world was round, not flat. Henry Ford was ridiculed for his prediction that automobiles would replace horse-drawn carriages. Steve Jobs was fired from Apple, the company he co-founded, because his vision for the company's future was deemed unacceptable at the time. Wow! This is it, so…

- Be unreasonable and expect unreasonable results.
- Run faster today because you can.
- Be more authentic and transparent today because your uniqueness is your gift to the world.
- Share your love for life today because when you smile, others get to see their own joy through you.

Never underestimate the power of your showing up authentically and enthusiastically. Face your greatest fear NOW! It is in *your* moment of true decision that all obstacles crumble before you. Look inside for your guidance and direction, for everything that you need to accomplish or create—because whatever you want and need already exists within you. It's like a cool feature on your computer or in your car that you never knew existed, even though it was always there just waiting for you to discover and use it.

Go ahead, transform yourself. Then be willing to transform yourself again tomorrow. Sameness and consistency can be great things, but only if you love where you are. Too often we create and cling to rules in order to satisfy our desire for certainty and comfort. But you are always *at choice*. That means that if you want, you can choose whether or not to be hypnotized into being simply the accumulation of your past habits, patterns and limitations and the aggregate of the expectations of other people. Or you can make a different choice. Often, it can seem to us that it is best to continue down the path that we already know so well, just because we know it so well. It is this familiar path, however, and staying on the path just because we know it so well that comes with a high cost.

The toll taken on your potential is huge when you give into your limiting beliefs and give up on your dreams and, as a result, never break through to see what life could be like on the other side of those limiting beliefs. Dismantle them! The other side is where real passion and zest reside, and it waits for you right now. *Right now*, in this and every future moment, is your chance to shatter your own outdated beliefs and start life fresh and new with the power of your own self-determination and resolve.

Trust me, the ultimate toll is not death… for death is just a part of the experience of life. The ultimate toll is paid by those who live their lives in neutral and never get out on the highway to see how fast they can go. This is it, my friend! *You've got this!* Today cries out for you to live it full out. You can start any aspect of your life all over again starting right now—fresh and as if you were showing up for the first time. The only thing that matters is what you do from this moment forward. The past, *your past*, is largely irrelevant when it comes to creating your future.

In every moment you have the choice to
drop the baggage that hindered you in the past!

The exciting thing is that there is a natural way of being that is uniquely yours to embrace. I don't know what that is for you—but *you* do! You are not here to fit in, but rather to express your unique gifts. Every time you choose to silence your true voice, to muzzle your powerful message and instead settle for just fitting in, you are cheating yourself and everyone that you meet.

Until you overpower any faulty, limiting beliefs that you have chosen to carry, you will never live the life that you came here to live— the life that represents your true gift and destiny. Make today a pivotal time when you discard the possibility that limiting beliefs hold power over you.

The good news is that if you are reading this book, you are definitely not here on this planet to fit in! You are here to stand out, to contribute your unique gifts, perspectives and insight. So many people have allowed themselves to mute the direction, the advice, the insight, the brilliance and the creativity that they possess in an effort to find acceptance—and fit in.

Does any of this sound or feel at least a bit risky? Excellent! Here is some great news. There is something that is always with you that has your back, especially when you climb out on what appears to be the skinny branches. The universal and connecting energy has your back.

I have come to know that through the universal energy, we are *always* connected, protected, guided and loved. When you remain in touch with your core and your purpose—who you came here to be—the events of any given day can never shake you. At the same time, if you disconnect from your core and let your anxiety-ridden thoughts prevail, you will inevitably feel separate, alone, defensive and powerless.

In my experience as a personal and business transformation coach, I have met so many fantastic people who had simply settled—whether in their life, or career, or both. In some cases, they had been driven and deeply dialed into their connection, but lost it along the way. Others simply didn't believe they ever had a real connection—at least, not like the energetic and vibrant people they most admire and want to emulate. Many of these folks had come to actually accept that they were just average, run-of-the-mill people and had unhooked from the idea that they had access to passion. Any chance you feel that way?

I'll tell you what I tell them: *Hell no!* Shake those thoughts off and move on. Because the truth is that your passion exists; it's strong and is freaking out that you haven't yet come to call on it. It may be hard to see because you've chosen to hide it under so many layers in order to avoid its call. But trust me, it is there. Whether you feel it right now or not, believe it—*you've got this!* You can stay bonded to it, or if you feel disconnected and have lost touch with your passion recently and need a little help reconnecting with it, this book will help. In this book, you will find the tools to destroy the tired, draining old thoughts and disempowering beliefs that have held you in a stranglehold. Rest assured, you have the ability to change the inner wiring that's held you in a disempowering holding pattern. How? By changing your beliefs to reflect the *truth*, not what your frightened mind (*aka, your ego*) has concocted to keep you playing and living small.

Let's look at this thing that we refer to as "ego" for a minute. I want to make sure that this is really clear because "ego" has different definitions in different cultures. Its roots are in Latin, where it means "I." In its purest form, ego is simply an acknowledgment that there is a "me," that there is something identifiable and assigned to "me."

This acknowledgment is a useful distinction to help us explore and understand our role in the world and bring context to our interactions with the environment and with other people. The ego energy that I am talking about, however, is one of the biggest derailers in our efforts to create, stretch, grow and make the dreams in our heart actually happen.

How crazy is it that arguably the single biggest obstacle to your achieving success and fulfillment is not some external condition but, instead, something that you have allowed to develop internally and have granted power to year after year? Yikes! Good news, though. It is only you who are in a position to give or deny power to this thing called your ego. You can master your ego; in fact, it is imperative that you do. You see, your ego is determined to hold you to the status quo, to playing small, to playing it safe, to shrinking back. Your ego will try to assert itself as that voice in your thoughts that says things like, "What are you thinking? You won't ever make that happen." *or* "You are out of your league, get real." *or* "Come on, man, if you try that, you are going to fail just like you always do. Play it safe. Don't set yourself up to be humiliated."

As loud as that internal naysayer can get—and that voice can get really loud—please, please, please remember that your ego voice has no inherent power; in fact, it only exists on the power that YOU give it. Each of us has this ego voice. But Warriors are committed to put ego in its place and grant it no power over them. You will learn how to become your own version of a Warrior in the pages that follow, and when you do, everything becomes possible.

Whether it is time to finally kick into a higher gear or simply time to reactivate and re-engage, the concepts that you will read about here will accelerate you and create the momentum that you need. There are five foundational components included in this model for creating a ridiculously fun, impactful, fulfilling life. In each chapter, we will take a deep dive into one of the five components of this success model. They include:

- Being grateful
- Being a Warrior
- Mastering resiliency
- Reinventing yourself again and again… *and again*
- Learning how to trust and let go

How do I know that these work? Not only have I implemented this model in my own life, but I have had the privilege, through my coaching engagements, to witness first-hand the powerful transformation these concepts have fostered in the lives of other people from countries around the world.

Here's the deal: For this to work for you, you have to be open to making a change in what you have held to be "true." We all work very hard to support the case that our view of the world is the right and valid one. But many times, our biggest springboard to personal growth comes when we are willing to release our tight grip on what we have believed to be true and open ourselves to the idea that there may be a better way for us to process and integrate things as we move forward. Beliefs that have served you well in the past may not serve you well in the future—for you are a different person now than when you first adopted them. You see, no matter what you actually do for a living, the reality is that you are in the belief-changing business—and your first customer is YOU. Change out old, tired, ineffective beliefs. Change your results and you will change your future!

The key concepts we will be working with will help you regain a strong sense of confidence, allow you to feel way more comfortable taking big risks, and help you get back into the flow of success—and enjoy the massive rewards that follow. There are five practices that are particularly important to master, because as you do, you will become a more powerful person and the world will respond. You see, we are continuously training others, including our family, friends, and co-workers, how to treat us by what we allow, what we nurture, what we expect, what we tolerate, what we support, what we will stand up for—and what we will not stand for.

In a similar way, we also "train" the universe how to treat us. When we choose to play small, think small thoughts and settle, then the universe responds much like a genie in a bottle granting you exactly what you put your energy on. It will conspire to help us create a path that leads toward a small life—or it can do just the opposite. Amazingly enough, and even though it will happen at the subconscious level, other people and the universal energy will support whatever thoughts and beliefs you internalize and project. YOU are the determining factor in the life and results that you create—no one and nothing else.

I believe that deep down, we all have a "knowing," an awareness that we are in fact connected, protected, guided, and loved. It's built into our DNA. But sometimes things happen in our lives that can bury and disconnect us from this important understanding. Some of us have had tough, even traumatic, experiences as children and throughout our lives that can bury this understanding—and as a result, we no longer feel safe.

The truth is that you ARE still safe. You were built to test your abilities and you cannot truly fail. There is always a safety net under you—*especially* when you are stepping out of your comfort zone and taking chances. You will soon see that when you radiate the knowing that you are connected, protected, guided and loved, the universe will open and respond with exactly what you need at exactly the right time. Therefore, when each of us…

- Lives from a place of deep gratitude, more and more things show up in our lives to be grateful for.

- Commits to be a Warrior and to be brave and bold and courageous, we naturally inherit more exciting challenges and opportunities.
- Masters the skill of resiliency, we teach the universe that we are unstoppable—and in return, become supported in our ability to bounce back from setbacks with optimism, hope, confidence and determination.
- Becomes open to reinventing ourselves again and again *and again*, the universe recognizes that we are ready to experience as much as possible in this lifetime, and more and more opportunities to expand show up.
- Finally learns to trust and let go, the universe stands even more ready to shoulder part of the burden that we previously felt certain we must carry alone.

So, take the leap! Come on… "Leap and the net will appear," as the Zen saying tells us.

I wrote this book to share what I have learned during my own personal journey—and to wake you up and shake you up—to insist, if I may be so bold, that you start to actually *live* the amazing life that you have been given. I'm committed to making sure that you dig in and never lose your passion, ever! The five concepts I have just described will show you how.

You've got this! means that if you choose, you can and will deliberately create your future, never again losing your passion, drive, and power. It means staying directly connected to your inner guidance and to the universal energy that always supports you.

Is it time to step up—to step back into being the leading man or leading woman in the creation of your amazing life and future? Are you ready to live full out and not be left out? Are you *sure*? Excellent!

You've got this—so let's do it!

Chapter 2

Be Grateful for You are Connected, Protected, Guided and Loved

L et me guess. You're reading this book because you've finally decided not to waste any more time. For the balance of your time on Earth, you're determined to live large, live it all up and reap the rewards—and ultimately the fulfillment—that come when you dig in and go for what you want on a sustained basis. This is it. No more fooling around. Life's too short, and you want to have more, do more, contribute, create and make an impact at a higher level. Each of us has our own priorities—but just wondering, is it safe to say that you are ready to...

- Attract friends that are inspired, inspiring, fun, smart, and just simply amazing?
- Have a ton of money? It's OK, that doesn't mean you're greedy. After all, dollars are really just "Fun Tickets" that give you access to jump on life's many rides, have great experiences, enjoy your life and give to others along the way.

- Make an amazing and positive impact on the lives of other people, those that are close to you as well as those that you may never actually meet?
- Leave a legacy of excellence and be an example to all of a life well lived?

What shifts will you make that shut down the "Maybe someday I'll go for it" circuit and activate the "*GAME ON!*, get out of the way, I'll handle it!" circuit? I have found that people often move through periods of their lives, going through the motions, but with some really important circuits shut down and out of commission. With these circuits out of service, it is easy to lose track of their goals and mission. Clarity and direction falter. Their powerful internal GPS system that's designed to let them know when they are on the right or wrong track fails. With these circuits down, connection to their natural wisdom and intuition becomes muffled or even silenced altogether.

Now that you've decided to switch your power circuits back on... *you're* on, *you've got this!* The new tools and ideas that you access here will lead to the practice of powerful new habits. Powerful new habits lead to strong results, and as you experience the excitement of these, you'll notice that your expectation of what is possible will expand. You will feel something other than "Maybe someday I'll go for it." You'll move fully into *"I've Got This!"* mode.

This chapter is an invitation to move into that kind of positive expectation right now. This book is different from others that you might have read. As an example of that difference, right out of the gate, I'm going to ask you to temporarily unhook from your ambitions, goals, strategies and desires—and invest your complete attention in dialing up your level of gratitude—day in and day out, in each and every moment.

Why? Because I have come to understand that gratitude is the foundation on which all success is built. In the chapters that follow, I'm going to introduce you to various components of success, but none of them will have an ounce of worth unless you first implement a consistent practice of deliberate gratefulness

There are several expressways to success that only open in the presence of gratitude. Great accomplishment starts with gratefulness. Whether expressed as faith, acknowledgement of the contributions of others, prayer or affirmations, gratitude anchors to a belief that people, things and energy all have roles to play in helping us find what we seek.

Gratitude is an inside-out phenomenon. Your level of gratitude does not rely on the conditions of your life. You are free at any moment to let go of fear and worry and simply replace those heavy thoughts with the lightness and peace that come with gratitude. This is not a concept that I just cooked up—it's ancient, consistent and universal.

> "Gratitude is not only the greatest of virtues, but the parent of all others."
> —Cicero (106 BC – 43 BC), Pro Plancio, 54 BC

Defining Gratitude

Let's step back for a second and take a look at what "gratitude" really means. Webster's dictionary defines gratitude as "a feeling of appreciation or thanks". We can do better than that definition, though.

Researcher Robert Emmons writes, "Gratitude is an affirmation of goodness. We affirm that there are good things in the world, gifts and benefits we've received."

Sociologist Georg Simmel refers to gratitude as "the moral memory of mankind."

I think of gratitude this way: Gratitude is an acknowledgement and celebration of what shows up in your life. It's an appreciation of the lessons that all events and people that you have met have helped you learn. It's a joyful acceptance that each experience, even those we see as challenging, is accompanied by an even greater gift that allows us to enjoy our life more outrageously, while discovering who we really are.

When you enter any situation from a foundation of gratitude, an additional connection is made between your conscious thinking brain and your heart and soul. Why is this important? Because within your heart live some of the most powerful elements for creating and living life according to your own definition of extraordinary. In your heart, your intuition, guidance and inherent wisdom are standing ready to guide you and to keep you on the path to results and the accomplishment of your mission in life.

Quite simply, gratitude is the springboard from which you elevate virtually every aspect of your life.

Gratitude Illustrated

An elderly woman sat calmly in the waiting room of the assisted living facility where she was to live out her remaining days. Her name was Betty. Her husband of seventy years had just passed away and, given her physical condition, moving to assisted living was the next logical step.

She waited over an hour while her room was being prepared. Finally a nurse entered the waiting room and beckoned for Betty to walk with her. Making small talk, the nurse mentioned that they'd just hung new lace curtains over the windows in the woman's room. As they continued down the hall, Betty smiled and said, "This is wonderful! The room is just perfect."

"Well, wait a minute," the nurse replied. "You haven't even seen it yet."

It was in this moment that the nurse's education began.

This wise elderly woman then said, "My happiness or unhappiness doesn't have to do with new curtains or the color of the walls. It's not how the furniture is arranged—it's how I've arranged my mind. I can complain or be frustrated or sad about the parts of my body that no longer work, or I can be grateful for the parts that still work well for me. I can choose to be sad that I have left the home that I raised my family in, or I can choose to be grateful for the fact that there is a place like this for me to stay now. I've already decided that I'm going to love my room. I will enjoy my time here, reliving all the great memories I've saved up for this time of my life."

What a powerful and beautiful approach to life! Betty shows us how a focus on gratefulness transforms challenging and difficult times into experiences of growth and deepening appreciation. When I hear of people living immersed so deeply in gratitude for what *is*, and not whining and complaining about what *is not*, I am humbled by their example. Not only does gratitude make us feel good emotionally and spiritually, it makes us feel good physically also. Let's have a look.

The Physical Effects of Gratitude Thinking

Several years ago, I became consumed by one question: What differentiates people who create massive success and joy from those who settle for just getting by?

I thought if I could solve that one mystery, I'd hold in my hands the key to both abundance and real happiness. I already had an inkling of what worked, but I started doing some homework to see if I was on the right path. This is what I found:

During my research, I came across separate studies conducted by researchers at the University of Pennsylvania, the University of California at Davis, the University of California at Berkeley, and Harvard University—all on the topic of the benefits of a deeper appreciation for what we have and what we experience. Each of these studies pointed toward a single conclusion: When a person consciously shifts their focus to *gratitude*, the results are overwhelmingly positive, powerful, significant and measurable.

Here are just some of the amazing results that were obtained when study participants made an attitudinal tweak to their daily routines and practiced feeling more grateful:

- Blood pressure and pulse rates decreased, creating better health in both the short-term and long-term, resulting in less wear and tear on their bodies.
- Cortisol, a stress hormone that is released to produce the "fight or flight" response, decreased, allowing for better strategic decisions.
- Endorphin levels increased, creating a sense of mental and emotional calm, connectedness and well-being.
- Muscle tension decreased, allowing for better circulation, accelerated healing and reduced pain.
- Immune system health improved dramatically, resulting in fewer sick days.
- Depression-resistant and anxiety-resistant brain activity increased.
- Faster recovery from major medical challenges such as a heart attack and a reduced probability of recurrence.

… and those were just the *health* benefits!

Gratitude also negates negative, toxic emotions that can cause depression, such as envy, resentment and regret. It turns out that you can't be both envious and grateful at the same time. They are incompatible feelings.

Gratitude, appreciation, fear and frustration all literally *change your body chemistry*—obviously, some for the better, some for the worse. These studies validated what I'd suspected all along. When we have an active focus and appreciation for what we already possess and what is already in place supporting us, we actually radiate gratitude and attract more into our lives to be grateful for.

On the other hand, when we find ourselves immersed in fear, frustration or lack, we attract more to be fearful, frustrated and resentful about. Gratitude and appreciation place you on an upward-bound spiral that leads to more and more of what you want. Fear and frustration place you on a downward spiral leading to more and more (*you guessed it*) pain and disappointment.

If you are always waiting for the other shoe to drop, it will! These spirals are always turning—always. And you are either embracing or initiating an upward or downward one. You know the drill, sometimes if a day starts off bad, it just gets worse and worse. You are racing out the door and accidentally spill coffee on your white shirt, then there's a wreck on the freeway and traffic backs up, then a co-worker calls in sick on the very day that you needed him most. And have you also noticed that sometimes days that start off great just keep getting better?

So what can you do about it? Change it—by deliberately changing your focus? Sure, I know you've heard this before, but it's the *way you choose to view things* and the way you choose to respond to events, that make the difference in the results that you get.

This is where the simple concept of gratitude comes in. It creates a whole paradigm shift. By switching to gratitude mode, you will look through a different lens at whatever is happening—and you can then step back and make a decision about how you are going to perceive it and respond to it. In short, your perception changes things. It changes *you!* The dynamic is pretty amazing.

In my life, I've experienced both sides of this crazy "gratitude-versus-lack" coin. Perhaps you have too. There were definitely periods in my life when I spent a lot of my time and attention on what I *didn't* have and on why I didn't get a fair shake.

When I was in my early teens, certain thoughts circulated through my mind on a seemingly endless loop. *How come my friends have cooler clothes and nicer cars than I do? Why are other kids more popular? Why do the cute girls want to kiss those other guys and not me? Why were other kids' parents still married while mine were divorced? What did I do to make my dad leave?* Lack, lack, lack! It may be hard to believe, but when I was growing up in Denver, I was the only kid I knew whose parents were divorced. That made the situation more difficult.

I was tall and lanky early on and I hated it. I tried everything I could think of to downplay my height and be more like the "normal" kids. While I just wanted to fit in, where was my focus? I looked at the attributes of others with envy and consistently felt that I didn't stack up. Damn, that felt terrible. But I didn't know how to change that awful feeling of "less-than-ness."

In recent years I've talked with old friends and classmates, and interestingly, many of the people I envied in those early days say that they envied me and felt that they were the ones that were awkward and on the outside looking in.

In a similar way, in less secure moments of my young adulthood, I found myself repeating the same mental patterns. *Why do I have to work so hard while others seem to breeze through their workloads?* So much of my energy was consumed with comparing myself to other people—what they had, how they were, what they did or did not do. It was exhausting.

As country singer Jake Owens puts it, "We all want what we ain't got!" When we are not coming from a place of gratitude, we tend to devalue our own talents and gifts and wish we had more of the attributes we see in others.

Let me give you an example of what I'm talking about. I spent a big part of my career in sales and marketing roles within companies that provided very technical, engineered solutions for the energy industry. It turned out that I was really successful and was always a top sales producer. I could strike up a conversation with anybody and feel comfortable, even energized, in a crowded association meeting or in front of the room leading a sales presentation. The success was fun and rewarding, but I noticed something interesting. Deep down, I often felt inferior to the engineers who had great analytical skills and technical proficiencies. I envied their intellectual capabilities and wished that I had their skills. In those moments, my focus was on what they had that I didn't have—not on valuing and appreciating and being grateful for the skills and abilities that I had.

It turned out that, at the same time, the engineers I worked with admired me for my ability to communicate, build relationships, be at ease with other people, and win new business. We all want what we ain't got *until* we make the shift from lack, envy and "less-than-ness" to gratitude and appreciation. Comparing ourselves to others, while a natural thing to do, can be phenomenally and unnecessarily destructive and derailing.

We'll talk about healthy and unhealthy comparisons later in this chapter. For now, though, I invite you to consider that most of the comparisons we indulge in stem from and perpetuate lack, insecurity, and a feeling of separateness. They make us feel less powerful, whole, perfect, and complete. Comparison is a four-letter word. (*OK, not really, but it should be!*)

I didn't want to live within that negative and disempowering energy long-term. I knew I would never become the person I wanted to be with my focus on what I *didn't* have. So I set out to find the answer to letting go of unhealthy comparisons that led to negative feelings. I needed a fundamental change in my approach. As I began an intentional, daily practice of deliberately placing my attention on what I *did* have in my life, my life changed—and became truly magical.

This one simple shift can bring more happiness and success to your life, too. Let's look at how this principle applies to business and the workplace.

Steve's Big Shift

Steve owns a multi-million-dollar business. The success of his business is reliant on the ability of his five-person team to provide a very high level of customer service, a level of service that Steve is totally committed to delivering… period.

Steve knows his industry. He's also an excellent salesman with a genuine concern for the happiness of his customers. He handles all sales activities for his company and routinely overloads his team with work from the large number of transactions he brings in.

When I met him, Steve was consumed by frustration. He found himself consistently disappointed by what he saw as a lack of commitment and low energy from everyone on his team—everyone except himself. "Why can't everyone else on this team deliver at the same level I do?" he complained. Then he confessed, "What I really want is a bunch of robots that will do *exactly* what I ask, do it well, and have it done either early or on time."

Day in and day out, Steve was keenly aware of, and subconsciously looking for, evidence that his team had once again let him down. Fun place to work, right? This naturally led to more disappointment and frustration.

Of all the emotions humans have, frustration and disappointment in someone else are two of the most difficult to hide. Rolling eyes, big sighs, the silent treatment, occasional outbursts. Think about a time when someone important to you—your mom, dad, sports coach or boss—was disappointed in something you had done or not done that you were supposed to. No matter what they said or did to try to hide their disappointment, you felt it completely, right? Everyone on Steve's team experienced that gut-wrenching sense that he thought their work ethic was sub-par, that they were "C" players at best. Meanwhile, Steve wondered, "What's the point in firing these people, when any replacement I could find would probably be just as bad?"

To get Steve's company on the track to sustainable growth and to reverse the high turnover rate on his team, something had to shift—and the shift had to happen within Steve.

It was easy for him to place the ownership of poor performance on his team. By doing so, he'd lulled himself into the somewhat comfortable belief that he was powerless, a victim of this circumstance. He grew more frustrated and disappointed with each passing day, and because of his negative focus, he was met with more things to be frustrated and disappointed about.

If Steve had continued down the path of frustration and disappointment, he would have likely destroyed his company, while the whole time blaming his team, not himself. In our work together, we focused on shattering his long-held notion that other people didn't care as much as he did.

Eventually he took ownership of the poor situation, and over a period of time, the energy and dynamic of his team changed. He worked hard to create a new mindset, one in which he tabled his past reaction of frustration and disappointment in his team and, instead, started looking for things to admire in each person—things he could actually be grateful for.

Steve figured something out. When he repeatedly anchored himself to the belief that his team was going to let him down, they did. And when he repeatedly anchored himself to a belief that his team would pull through and perform well, they did.

He successfully shifted his expectation from things to be frustrated about, to things to be grateful for. Today, Steve and his team are completely synched up and are the dominant force in their market. The team alignment that was always available, just waiting for Steve to shift his approach, was now producing not only improved financial results but also a fun and energizing place to work, contribute and grow. He's now enjoying better idea-generation, stronger company morale, faster execution, and improved revenue and profits—all of it because of a switch in attitude and a switch to gratitude.

In Every Moment, There's a Choice

So let me guess, your interest is piqued and you want to know what it would take to make a similar shift in your approach, one that will connect you more strongly to your natural state of ease and clarity—one that will move you from frustration and disappointment to gratitude and appreciation. You're thinking, "Sounds awesome, Will, sign me up! So where do I begin?"

Begin with the realization that in every moment of your life, you have a CHOICE. You can choose to either focus on what you have, or focus on what you don't have. Gratitude is an option that's always available to you, and it can be turned on as easily as it can be turned off.

In every moment, we stand at a crossroads. As we choose and move forward on one path, we simultaneously reject the other. The key differentiator here is whether we chose to be grateful and attached to our heart or frustrated and disappointed in ourselves and others and attached to our whiny ego.

Gratitude is a simple matter of choice. It is by no means the only option. Any of us can, and many of us do, choose by default to become more and more hardened, closed off and resentful—more and more frustrated and disappointed, wondering why we got the short end of the stick. It is always right within our grasp, though, to deliberately embrace a simple lifelong regimen that opens us up to create and receive more by making gratitude our default setting. Just having the ability to deliberately choose your attitude and mindset is incredibly empowering—and is something in and of itself to be very grateful for.

Start now! Don't wait for the next thing you want to show up so that you can then be grateful for it. It works the other way around—especially if you are struggling or feeling sorry for yourself. This is the exact time to let go of those worn out stories and… *GET GLAD IN THE SAME SHOES YOU GOT SAD IN!*

Three Keys to Getting on the Grateful Track

Here are three easy things that you can bring to the forefront of your thinking that'll help you establish a deeper and more replicable habit of gratitude:

- *Keep looking for the gift.* With every adversity, there comes a gift. Look for the gift in your circumstances and emotions, especially the ones that feel confusing. Perhaps the gift or lesson is simply that it's okay to let go and let the universe drive for a while. I have a note taped to my desk where only I can see it. It simply says, "Look for the gift." This little sticker reminds me of this important principle and helps me be disciplined in directing my focus whether things are going well or not so well.

- *Compared to what?* When you're focused on your problems, it is common for them to expand and for you to see them as bigger than they actually are. Let me ask you something. As real as any problem or challenge that you are facing right now is, and I acknowledge that you might be facing some very difficult times, is it really as insurmountable as you're making it out to be? How does your challenge compare to those of the millions of people on our planet who won't have anything to eat today? Tough times? I feel ya! But tough times compared to what? In relative terms, your life is good right now, today. What would you have to believe or notice in order for you to be able to be grateful for your circumstances—both the good and the bad, for it is the combination of the good and the bad experiences that craft the fullness of life. Tell me again about your big problems… compared to WHAT?

- *Gratitude is about releasing!* Building your life on a foundation of gratitude means releasing—releasing comparisons, anger, gossip, struggle. Gratitude is your natural state, and it's the accelerator to attracting what you most want. It is in your very nature, in your DNA, to be grounded in gratitude. Whatever shows up in your day, whether it is something you view as a good thing or a bad thing, just say, "Perfect!" This response is an acknowledgement that whatever you're experiencing has shown up for a reason and is contributing to your greater good and to the greater good of those around you.

This includes feeling grateful for your lifestyle, your skills, and the friends and family that support (and sometimes stretch) you. It means appreciating the many things most people take for granted—like clean water for drinking, electricity to make life easier, the amazing landscape along your drive to work, and the financial and career opportunities that are simply yours for the taking. It's also an acknowledgement of the endless list of cool experiences you can choose to explore. And last but not least, it's a silent expression of thanks for the health and strength of your body and the gift of your brilliant mind.

Notice, too, that focusing on what you *don't* have knocks you out of the present moment. Your time reference shifts to either the past, where you will be tempted to anchor to all the reasons that you're a victim of your circumstances, or to the future, where you have the anxiety of not knowing if things will turn out the way you want them to.

The fact is, you can't change the past. And while you can certainly alter your future at any time, what makes positive change and advancement possible is the attitude you embrace and the actions you take in each and every *present* moment. When you are centered in gratitude, you automatically expand what is possible for you, right here and right now.

You must make that choice carefully—to focus on what you have or on what you don't have. Your choice has a profound effect on your energy, capacity, adaptability, productivity, attitude, and most importantly, your results.

You see, gratitude is a high-quality energy. When you exude high-quality energy, high-quality experiences and results will follow.

Callout: A Message for the Macho Men

All right, guys. I see some of you rolling your eyes. I know this stuff might sound a bit too delicate and fluffy, but making a continuous practice of gratitude takes guts and muscle. You have to work at this regularly if you want to see real results. The bigger your commitment to this practice of gratitude, the bigger your success will be. So don't sit it out on the sidelines with this one. It's too important.

PITFALLS TO WATCH OUT FOR

Keeping up with a consistent practice of gratitude isn't always easy, and this will initially require some discipline. Fortunately, like anything else, it gets easier with repetition.

Along the way, however, you'll run into a few obstacles, and most of those will be self-generated. The good news is that since you're the one that is creating the obstacles, that means you are also the one that has the power to destroy them. The following are three big ones to watch out for:

1) Feeling sorry for yourself?

Sometimes, in our efforts to feel significant, we place our focus on our problems. Why? Because when we're burdened with problems, we can complain to our friends and family about how hard we have it and how our daily path is so much more difficult than theirs. In some circles, being miserable has its advantages.

Misery loves company, and we all love to feel connected to those around us, but bonding through the sharing of complaints and problems is the laziest, lowest common denominator behavior.

While I mostly felt that I was a pretty grateful guy, until a few years ago, I hadn't been making a conscious decision to focus on my gratitude. Instead, I spent time feeling sorry for myself and sometimes allowed a vision of myself as a victim to prevail. The more I let people in on my challenges, the more they consoled me. While it felt good to get the attention… *what was I thinking?* Feeling *sorry* for myself? Wow! Let's face it—if you, like me, were lucky enough to be born in a stable, developed country, you have already won the lottery compared to millions of people on our planet who are currently displaced by famine and war.

But I don't need to waste your time contrasting all the things you have that so many others do not. You already know that you live a fortunate life and also have amazing attributes built into your very fiber, both physical and mental. You, my friend, are incredibly lucky, and you can accomplish ANYTHING. There are no limits and no exceptions to that. Now that's something to be grateful for!

So, no matter what you're experiencing right now—whether you're on top of the world or just barely hanging on, take a look around you. In reality, you're living in paradise. Instead of focusing on what you don't have, or what you think you need to be happy, identify all the things around you that are already in place, all the things that support you and make your life easier. Pity party? I don't think so!

2) Worried about rough weather ahead?

Many of us make a lifelong habit of worrying that things will go poorly in the future. As human beings, we have a basic desire to feel safe and protected, and in its own twisted way, our worrying mind is trying to keep us safe. But left unchecked, those unfounded fears will hold you back and keep you playing small in life. Waiting for the other shoe to drop creates and attracts what you don't want.

Remember this: Worry is a nasty habit and gratitude is the cure.

That's why it's so important to maintain your practice of gratitude in both good times and bad. When the waters ahead look rough, you may be tempted to worry about what is up ahead around the next bend. But that's when gratitude can help you the most. Shift your focus to what you have supporting you.

Also, when you think about it, you really don't need protecting. There is nothing you need to protect. The sense of protection you seek already exists. It's built into the fabric of who you are. I know that this may seem somewhat difficult to accept but here's the deal—you are always connected, protected, guided and loved. The truth is, you are protected just by your placement on Planet Earth, and wherever you are in this moment is exactly where you're supposed to be. *EXACTLY!*

As it turns out, your challenges are your greatest gifts. Consider this: If everything in life was just rolled out in front of you, requiring absolutely no effort on your part, what would that be like? Maybe it sounds great on the front end, but in reality, it would lead to an exceedingly boring life. What you cherish as great victories each time you overcome the odds would be replaced by only shallow wins.

So know that whatever is in front of you, whatever needs to be tackled, is present in your life for a reason. Perhaps it's there to help you grow, stretch, find new solutions, or tap into different parts of your creativity that you never knew you had. Who knows why that particular challenge has shown up just now? The truth is, "why" doesn't matter. What matters is the mindset we choose and our ability to openly embrace it and look for the lesson that it has shown up to teach us.

Remember that where you are RIGHT NOW is *EXACTLY* where you're supposed to be. Be grateful for what you are experiencing right now for it is the springboard to your desired future. Look for the gift. Step into that. When difficulties arise, ask yourself, "What emotion am I transmitting that attracted this?" and "Am I coming from a place of gratefulness or lack?"

Never forget that lessons will always cost more tomorrow than they do today. Be grateful for what is showing up in your life. Look for the gift in every challenge. Find the lesson.

3) Caught in the "Comparison Trap"?

Far too often, we chose to get caught up in comparing ourselves and our circumstances with others. This is a game that you will never win. Does any of the following sound familiar?

- I can't hold a candle to that guy; he's much smarter than I am.
- These other women are so much prettier and thinner than I am.
- He started out with advantages I didn't have, so I'll never go as far as he did.
- I'll never be able to accomplish what she's accomplished. I've missed my chance.
- He lives in a big city with lots of resources. I can't accomplish anything in this podunk town!
- She's so relaxed with people. I'm too shy to establish a network like hers.

I call this the Comparison Trap. It's human nature to compare yourself to others, but it's absolutely critical that you shun the "victim thinking" that comes from these disempowering kinds of comparisons.

The Comparison Trap is expensive. As you attempt to fit in and match the behaviors of others, you inevitably lose your own personality—your quirkiness, your uniqueness and your individuality. That's a hefty cost, because these are the very gifts that will make you powerful and impactful.

Whenever you begin to feel off-balance or caught up in worry about who-has-what compared to you, spring back to a solid foundation of gratitude. It's your fastest path back to the present moment, where all your power resides—and to peace of mind.

DO IT!

Imagine for a minute that you find yourself shipwrecked on a small tropical island. There is no one else with you. Suddenly, survival depends on your quickly figuring out how locate food and water, build shelter and maybe fend off predators. All that you focus on now is what you need to do to stay alive so you access your inventory of skills and tools—and then take action. Whether or not someone else could do what has to be done any better or not becomes completely irrelevant. You find that you have no need or ability to compare yourself or your ideas to anyone else's.

Now, travel back to your daily, real world environment. Even though there are likely many people all around you, there is still no value to wasting time comparing yourself to anyone else. PERIOD!

Seek out great mentors? Yes! Learn from the mistakes and successes of others? For sure! Comparison Trap? Hell No!

Move toward your goals with the skills, attributes, instincts and knowledge that you have onboard right now in this present moment. Professional distance runners have a mantra: "Run the mile that *you* are in." Don't concern yourself with what those around you are up to.

---

4) Believe you're just not programmed for happiness?

There is a great deal of information available in the research communities on the topic of "set points" for human beings—emotional, psychological, and physical. A set point is a state to which the body or mind wants to habitually return. The set point concept of body weight is an example. After rigorous dieting is abandoned, for instance, people often return to their body's pre-diet, "set point" weight.

However, research on gratitude has challenged the idea of a set point for happiness. Some believe that just as the body has a set point for weight, each person may also have a genetically determined set point for happiness.

Fortunately, this theory has been debunked. Several research studies cited in the American Psychological Association's publication, *Science Watch*, have concluded that people who engage in grateful thinking are able to sustain a greater level of happiness over the long haul—in other words, a new, higher happiness set point can be established.

> *Sustained Gratitude can actually reprogram your brain to seek out and find more happiness and joy*

Rick's Dilemma

Let me tell you a story about Rick. He is a friend of mine and a real estate investor who buys houses, fixes them up, and then sells them for a profit.

One beautiful day while Rick and I were riding on a ski lift in Vail, Colorado, he talked about his recent trials and tribulations with building contractors. Some of the contractors he'd hired over the past few years had over-promised and under-delivered, leaving him with one problem after another. As a result, he'd grown sick of the whole real estate business.

I asked him what it was he thought he might be doing to invite such unreliable workers time and time again—and what he thought he could do to turn around the string of disappointing interactions. "Damn it, Will, you asked me that same question six months ago!" he said. "I have been thinking about that and here's the reality. All of my friends in the real estate business have the same problems with contractors. What am I supposed to do, change the whole industry?"

I wasn't suggesting that he try to change a whole industry— only to change the experience *he* was having within the industry. I asked him a few more questions: "How explicit are you being about your expectations? Are you sure you're being completely clear about timelines, specific work, specific materials? Or are you just assuming that the contractors know what they're doing and should know what you're looking for?" In my experience, one of the most frequent and frustrating challenges for managers, business owners, spouses and parents is expecting that others should just know what we want and need. Instead of being clear and explicit, we stay unclear and then are frustrated when the other person comes up short on what they deliver.

Rick admitted that he hadn't been overly clear or specific about his expectations, in part because he felt it might be insulting to the contractors. They were professionals, after all. He saw the point, though, and decided to commit to stating his expectations with massive clarity for the next two months to see if it would lead to improved results.

We kept talking and I asked him to take a important gut check. "To what extent are you expecting your contractors to pull through for you, to dazzle you with their work and timeliness?" I asked. "And to what extent are you expecting them to let you down?" He thought for a minute, then told me he was entering each of these contracts with the core belief that they'd go poorly. He pretty much expected to be disappointed.

Next, I asked him if he felt he trusted me enough to make a commitment to work with the 21-day program I'd developed for starting each day with power and deliberateness (described in the next section). He replied that he not only trusted me, but that he would try *anything* if it had a shot at turning his business around. He then committed to say the following each morning for the next sixty days:

> *"As I enter into this new day, I do so fully expecting that all of those I interact with today will do what they say they will do and pull through for me in every way. I state this as my firm intention, supported in the knowledge that I am not a creature of circumstance, but rather the decisive element in the creation of my circumstances. My expectations influence my results."*

Rick and I touched base again after a couple of months, and here's what he had to say about his experiment: "It was amazing, a real eye-opener. I had no idea what just specifying my needs and expectations could mean in terms of smoothing out the work process." Then he joked, "Hey, I guess that's why they call them 'spec' homes, but at any rate, I now have a team I can work with, one that delivers reliable results and doesn't drive me crazy in the meantime. I don't know why I didn't do this earlier."

Rick's story exemplifies the power of positive expectation. It's extremely clear. *EXPECT* others to pull through for you. Say what you need to say, then expect a good outcome. (Bonus: You're business and personal relationships will become a lot more fun too.)

While you're examining this concept, ask yourself whether your expectations are *explicit* or *implicit*? If they are implicit, are you giving yourself an "out" by creating an excuse for lack of performance, like Rick was? This is a common pitfall.

We all experience frustrations and disappointments in life. For some, these negativities take root and become a primary area of focus—both externally, through conversations with others, and internally, through thoughts. When this happens, an energy field is created (sometimes referred to as an "aura"), that charges everyone and everything that it encounters with negativity associated with frustration and disappointment. In other words, the energy of others is shifted by the energy of those around them. This is a well-accepted law of physics and it works with both positive and negatively charged energy.

Your job is to build on a life of positive expectation. Develop an attitude of relaxed confidence and know that when you are engaged in work that you are truly meant for, the results that you are looking for will come to you more easily. Remember that it's your choice to be nervous or calm, to expect the worst or the best. Be deliberate about this. You will find, like Rick did, that in every moment you can transcend the challenges that confine most people. And as you do, you will experience amazing, *even magical*, changes in your life.

Inspect what you expect.
What is your primary focus and expectation?
Expect people to deliver for you and they will.

ACTIONABLE STEPS
For Replacing Fear, Frustration and Disappointment with Gratitude and Appreciation
In Just 21 Days!

Do you want to experience the life-changing benefits of habitual grateful thinking? Are you ready to gain control and consciously attract the strength and power you need to accelerate results in every aspect of your life?

You might be thinking, *"Of course, Will, who wouldn't want that kind of personal power? But it seems like such a massive change, and I'm afraid I'm fighting an uphill battle. I feel anchored in my old patterns of thinking. Where would I even begin to change?"*

I invite you to begin right here. I'm going to show you how to begin your new practice of grateful thinking—the same practice that transformed my life and continues to work for me each and every day. If you commit to the actions I suggest below, you will have replaced your fear and worry with gratitude and more happiness in just 21 days. That's right. Not years, not months, but *days!*

This is based on the neuroscience principle of Neuroplasticity, which has taught us that we can successfully reprogram our brain patterns and replace them with new connections that lead to new and different results. We have found that you can change the way you have historically processed information with this practice.

Keep in mind, however, that there's a difference between intellectually *knowing* you "should" be more grateful, and actually building a strong, repeatable process that initiates, then sustains your mindset of gratitude.

I know those negative thought patterns feel well worn. You can almost feel the ruts they've formed across your brain. But those patterns are 100% changeable by anyone, including you. Old patterns, even those that hold us back, are often kept alive because they become part of our mental and emotional safety zone. That transformation begins with one step, and continues with a daily practice. It will require commitment.

Here's how to get started with your exercises for anchoring this new way of approaching life:

YOU CAN START TODAY

Let's increase your level of happiness and gratefulness by starting to build that muscle right now. Look around. What things do you already have in your life that support you and make your life easier? List them—here are some ideas to get you going.

- Do you own a car that gives you the freedom and flexibility to go wherever you want to at any given moment?
- Do you have a refrigerator in your home that keeps food (*or beer!*) cold and fresh, ready for whenever you want it?
- Do you have heat in your home that keeps you warm on bitterly cold nights?
- Do you have talents that make it easier for you to do things others can't? For example, can you calculate rapidly in your head? Are you good with words? Do you have a quick and clever sense of humor? Are you a keen observer who picks up on details without effort?
- Do you have empathy, allowing you to connect easily with others? Do you have drive and determination? Intelligence? Intuition?

Now think of all the miraculous ways your body functions, without your having to think about it. Your blood circulates. Your eyes see. Your ears hear. Your skeleton holds you upright. Your muscles move you. Your lungs breathe. Cuts and scrapes heal themselves. The food you eat is converted to energy. Your brain interprets words on a page or computer screen into thoughts and ideas. Imperfections and all, the human body is phenomenal!

Now, list all the other ways your body and brain support you, day in and day out.

Morning Kick-Start:

Get a blank notebook and place it by your bed, along with a pencil or pen. This will become your personal Gratitude Journal.

The two pages at the end of this chapter are titled "Morning Meditation" and "Evening Meditation." Copies of these pages are available on our website www.mpgcoaching.com. Go to the website and print out these templates because you will need to use them.

Tuck the Morning Meditation and Evening Meditation pages inside the notebook at your bedside.

1. Set your alarm for tomorrow morning fifteen minutes earlier than you normally would. Hang in there with me! Soon you'll look forward to this way of starting your day every day.

2. As you first recognize that you are no longer asleep, do something to wake up your brain (such as counting backward from 100 to zero, repeating the alphabet skipping every other letter, etc.).

3. Next, grab your notebook and read the Morning Meditation page including the steps for accessing what you are grateful for in you past, present and future. It is important to pick different things that you are grateful for each day. Log them in your Gratitude Journal each day.

4. Set your intentions for the day. It is most powerful if your list of intentions for the day ahead includes both things that you will *do* and ways that you choose to *be* including your selected attitude, level of patience, commitment to kindness, etc. (Note: more detail on this process for deliberately creating the results that you want is available in the "Expanding the Glimpse Audio Program" available at www.mpgcoaching.com/products)

REMEMBERING GRATEFULNESS AS YOU PROGRESS THROUGH YOUR DAY:

Spend some time placing reminder notes in places you consistently find yourself each day. Also, it is a great idea to program digital reminders on your smartphone or computer. These will become your Focus Notes on which you write reminders about your intentions for the day—and can include your commitment to:

1. Look for the gift in each event, introduction and interaction.
2. Drop all comparisons.
3. Release from gossip, needless resistance, struggle, negative thoughts.

Once you have your Focus Notes and digital reminders in place, make it a habit to briefly pause each time you see one and reflect on something for which you are grateful. The idea is to get accustomed to routinely pausing several times a day to connect to your sense of gratitude. Until that becomes habitual, your notes and prompts can help remind you.

You might also choose several trigger moments each day to pause and think gratefully. For example, you might train yourself to reconnect with your mindset of gratitude each time you step into an elevator, get into your car, or before you take your first bite of lunch.

AS YOU GET READY TO END YOUR DAY AND DRIFT OFF TO SLEEP:

When you get into bed at night, pause before sleeping to:

1. Grab your journal and list the 3 to 5 things that you are now grateful for as a result of living this day.
2. Read the Evening Meditation page you tucked inside your notebook.
3. Reflect on your successes while answering the questions included in the Evening Meditation.

This is the process for transforming the fear, doubt and worry into gratitude. As you deploy this, you are on your way to great results, more clarity and more enjoyment of life.

Do this simple and powerful exercise every day for 21 days—and you'll be astounded by your performance, results, and increased level of happiness! As Jim Rohn said so many years ago, "Success leaves clues." What you have just read is the aggregation of what almost every single mega successful person does in some form or another. So if you want to create the kind of results that they have created, mimic their daily habits. This is a great place to start.

MORNING MEDITATION

<u>STEP 1</u>: Take three deep breaths, drawing air in through your nose with your mouth closed. Hold each breath for four seconds, then exhale slowly through your mouth. Use a breathing pattern as follows: Inhale for 4 seconds, hold for 6 seconds, exhale for 8 seconds. Allow yourself to become more and more present and move into a deep state of thankfulness. Then read this:

Today, I make conscious choices.
I choose gratefulness and set aside jealousy.
I choose to create and set aside drama.
I choose to acknowledge my strength and set aside negative self-talk.
Today, I activate my ability to decide.
I have decided to be grateful for what I have.
I have decided to expect amazing results.
I have decided that I am unstoppable.
Today, I let go.
I let go of the need to control and embrace every experience that this day
holds for me.
I let go of the background chatter and embrace the wisdom of the voice
from my heart.
I let go and trust.
We are all connected, protected, guided and loved!
I commit to be more grateful today…

STEP 2: Reflect on the people, things or circumstances that have been part of your past for which you are grateful.

- What are the experiences—both the great ones and the tough ones—that made you the person you are today?
- Who are the people who've guided you? Who mentored you?
- Who tormented you—but as a result, pushed you to grow, stretch, get better?
- Who helped you set a new standard for your life?
- What in-born traits or qualities do you possess that helped make some things easy for you?

Write one or more of your responses in your notebook.

STEP 3: Reflect on the people, things, or circumstances for which you are grateful in your present life.

- What can you be grateful for that is part of your experience right now, today?
- What makes your life amazing?
- What have you been taking for granted? *Hint: It's pretty cool that all you have to do is flip a switch on your wall to have light, music, heat or AC in your room!*
- What do you love about your career?

Write one or more of your responses in your notebook.

STEP 4: Picture the things you want in your future. But instead of merely seeing them in your mind's eye, really *feel* the gratefulness. Accept that your vision of the future is 100% possible and feel deep appreciation. Remember: Gratitude transcends your mind. It's not a thought, it's an *emotion*. This is the secret to manifesting the life of your dreams. *See* it and *feel* it.

Write in your notebook one or more things that will be in your future for which you feel grateful.

Near the end of your life when all the pressure is off, you may experience a sense of gratitude for the many beautiful experiences you had along the way. Doesn't it make sense to live each day with that energy of gratitude, rather than saving it all up for the very end?

Gratitude is the foundation of bravery. Once gratitude propels you, you become unstoppable. Once gratitude fills your heart, fear is eliminated.

Now, with this connection to gratitude in place, get in the game and build your day to your high standards!

Never settle!

EVENING MEDITATION

STEP 1: Take three deep breaths, drawing air in through your nose with your mouth closed. Hold each breath for four seconds, then exhale slowly through your mouth. Use a breathing pattern as follows: Inhale for 4 seconds, hold for 6 seconds, exhale for 8 seconds. Feel the rhythm of your relaxed breathing style. Allow yourself to become more and more present and move into a deep state of thankfulness. Then read this:

Gratefulness is the key to peace of mind.
Gratefulness is the catalyst for joy.
Gratefulness is the magnet attracting to me all that I desire to experience.

STEP 2: Ask yourself:

- Where did I consciously choose to create, to be grateful, to acknowledge my strengths?
- Where did I decide to expect amazing results—and believe that I am unstoppable?
- At what points did I let go and really trust that I am connected, protected, guided and loved?
- What did I do today that moved me closer to my goals and desires, even just a little bit?
- Who gave me their time and energy today?
- What came easily to me today?
- What made me smile today?

Now, get to sleep… you have a big day tomorrow!

Chapter 3

You Are a Warrior!
Be Brave, Bold
and Courageous

"Life shrinks or expands in proportion to one's courage."
—Anais Nin

Warriors consistently stand strong and stand up for the life and results they want. Warriors find a way to conquer fear in the face of challenge and to direct strong focus toward their objectives. To achieve the lifestyle and fulfillment that you want takes warrior-like mental, emotional, physical and spiritual conditioning. Incorporating the gratitude and attraction models from the previous chapter grounds you to your inherent connectedness and inner guidance, which is the absolutely essential first step in building the bulletproof, unstoppable momentum that it will take to reach your highest goals and fulfill your dreams.

As you continue to master those powerful tools, the next step is to build out your personal Warrior Commandments. Your Warrior

Commandments are your code of conduct, designed to help your keep your mind and energy focused day in and day out and to minimize distractions. You see, success is an inside-out experience. The extent of your ultimate success is not subject to outside variables such as the economy, your upbringing, level of education, or what other people think you are capable of. You will create in your life whatever you allow yourself to believe that you are worthy and capable of achieving. Read that line again. Now read that line out loud. It's that important.

In this chapter, we will identify and explore the power of the Warrior Commandments. They are comprised of the following elements:

- Choices, Decisions, Consequences
- Two Competing States of Mind
- Patterns that Create Success and Patterns that Create Frustration and Disappointment
- Attitude and Positive Expectation
- The Immense Power of Personal Leverage
- Rethink Your Rules—Comfort Zone Be Damned!
- Build Your Power-Boosting Environments
- Ignite Your Super Powers
- Heart
- Fear

By the way, being a Warrior is not about winning *against* someone else. It is about conquering your own image and beliefs about *you*. Remember, you are the ONLY one that can make the decision to live an amazing life—and you make that choice every day. Top performers are Warriors. Top performers don't always know *how* they are going to do something—they just believe *that* they are going to do it. This is the top performance belief system that makes great things happen.

YOU are the single decisive element that determines the quality of the experiences you will have in this amazing life. It's never what you CAN do, it's what you WILL do!

Warrior Commandment # 1: Choices, Decisions, Consequences

No matter what situation is showing up in your life today, at some point in your past you had several choices that you could choose from. You made a decision as to which option to embrace, and yes, not making a deliberate choice is absolutely a form of decision. That decision landed you in the place where you are right now. Let's look at an example. Each day you are faced with hundreds of choices about what you consume and what you do to create your level of fitness. From that huge population of choices and options, you make many decisions, the aggregate of which shapes your physical strength and well-being. Today you may make decisions to eat a salad or a pizza for lunch, to walk or grab a cab, to work out or watch you favorite team on TV. Each decision that you make will take you incrementally closer to or farther away from your health and fitness goals. The consequences of all of those small decisions may not be experienced until years later when your physical strength and good or bad health are called upon in the event of a heart attack or physical trauma.

Your results begin with your decisions. It's your *decisions*, not your conditions that determine your destiny. Guard the gates of your future experiences and results by having the dedication of a Warrior when it comes to making your decisions.

Warrior Code: Every decision counts!

Warrior Commandment # 2: Two Competing States of Mind

Let's look at another hugely important decision that you make over and over again. Throughout life, you will be tested and your resolve will absolutely determine the quality and level of fun, excitement and passion that you will experience. You are in battle and your mental and emotional conditioning is needed more in this battle than anywhere else in your life. You see, you may often feel torn between two competing states of mind—one calling you to go BIG and to go all in. This one creates a resounding reminder that you are bulletproof, that you are unstoppable, that you are prepared and ready to launch—that nothing is impossible for you. The second one is calling to you to fall back, to play small, to wait until later, to push back. Whichever one of these two competing states of mind is most developed and conditioned into your mindset will prevail. You are the one, in fact the *only one* that is in the position to choose which one of these two mindsets you will nurture and support. As long as you build a system for anchoring massive certainty to a positive, unstoppable state of mind, the distance between you and what you seek will continuously shrink.

Whatever you believe to be true, you will find evidence to support that belief as fact. If you choose to believe that you are brave, then you will begin to show up in the way that a brave person would show up—and get the results that a brave person would. If, on the other hand, you give in to small thinking, you will manifest the life and limited results that a small and frail thinker will have. We are continually manifesting and creating our lives directly from our vision of ourselves. Deep down, you are a Warrior. Bring that Warrior to the surface and amplify your impact and experience now. The bravery of Warriors is the acceptance that our disempowering stories don't have any power or authority over us. Your life starts and accelerates when you go all in.

When we condition a can-do, won't-be-denied state of mind, we will always enjoy far greater results than if we condition a shrink back and think small mindset. The battle between a determined and expansive mindset and a shrinking back mindset is very real. It is a competition with a distinct winner and a distinct loser. So which state of mind will win? That is up to you. It has been said that in negotiations, the person with the most certainty wins. The same is true with the development of your primary state of mind. Start becoming more and more aware of which mindset is getting the most airplay as you move through your daily routine. Listen for the clues.

Warrior Code: Mindset matters!

It boils down to this—are you all in, or are you out? Decide. Period. You must be more committed to your goal than you ever believed possible. It is a change of mindset from "Can I?" to "I Can!" and from "Will I?" to "I Will!" Keep in mind that what you choose to focus on and believe about yourself will manifest itself outwardly.

Warrior Commandment # 3: Patterns that Create Success and Patterns that Create Frustration and Disappointment

Early in my coaching career, I was part of the coaching team for a well-known personal development expert, while at the same time building my own coaching business. At one point, I was serving 59 separate people, one-on-one as their coach. It was an insane level of activity, but I loved it because I had the privilege of helping a lot of people and developing my own expertise in the coaching field. The other huge benefit that came with having individual coaching sessions with up to thirteen people in a day was that I was able to see that there are only so many patterns that we, as humans, run.

Whether a person that I was working with wanted to quit smoking, lose weight, run a marathon, start a business, get a promotion, find a person to share their life with or fulfill any other desire, I noticed that there were very similar approaches that can be taken. There were patterns that people were exhibiting that created and attracted the results they wanted most—and, just as importantly—there were certain patterns that created repeated frustration, disappointment, pain and failure.

It became evident that the clients who enjoyed successful outcomes had similar behaviors. They worked at increasing their self-empowerment, they focused on what they wanted, they had developed a core belief, an expectation, that they would be successful and that they would overcome the challenges that would most certainly show up. They were Warriors, determined to create.

As we mentioned earlier, top performers don't always know *how* they are going to do something—they just believe *that* they are going to do it. They live anchored to their personal standards every day, not just when they feel like it. They consistently tack their identities to their strong values, not to their fears or doubts.

On the flip side, those clients who came to coaching almost as a last ditch effort, tended to share a different set of patterns at the outset—patterns which, left unchecked, had been templates for failure. They tended to tack their identities to their shortcomings, questioned their worthiness for success and happiness, and looked back on their lives with the spotlight on the times that things didn't go their way, people didn't pull through, or when they came up short. As painful as it is, people sometimes get stuck mentally, running from a past ghost that isn't there— giving away their power to negative energies and past put-downs. Consequently, they concoct story after story about why they "CAN'T".

Warrior Code: "Can't" is NOT part of your vocabulary.
Declare what you want with clarity
and fully expect it to show up.

Now, let's take a look at some of the mental and emotional processing patterns that create or destroy potential.

Filters

Your filters are the lens through which you experience the world. Since our brains can't possibly process all of the information that is available to us, we are constantly determining which data to bring to the attention of our conscious minds and which to ignore. Like a very high-speed computer processor, our brain is sorting and separating out the information that might be important for us to be aware of from the mass of data that is deemed not relevant or valuable. In order to get a sense of this filtering process, take a few seconds right now to become aware of all of the information, data and stimuli in your environment in just this present moment. As you increase your awareness, notice how you become aware of a whole new set of sounds; things that you could look at, such as the various colors in the room; physical sensations, such as the air moving past your skin and the feel of your clothes on your skin; sensations within your body, such as muscles that are relaxed or tensed. Add to this list the fact that we have more than 60,000 thoughts moving through our brains every day, and you'll quickly realize how important this filtering process is. Within our brain we have something called the Reticular Activating System (RAS) that is responsible for this filtering.

While the Reticular Activating System functions at the subconscious level and helps keep us sane, the filtering that I am referring to here is initially a distinctly conscious function and helps keep us productive and focused. Building a resolve to be more proactive in what you allow in and what you do *not* allow into your consciousness is a pattern of behavior that gives you a huge advantage because it increases your ability to stay on course and spend far less time sidetracked or derailed.

Here's an example: A few years ago I was working on a sales team for a large telecommunications company. A friend and coworker of mine flew into my office and said, "Man, did you hear what Bob was saying about the new competitors hitting the market? He is convinced that we're screwed." I looked up at my friend and said, "He may be right or he may be wrong, but as for me, I am not going to internalize that." From my friend's expression, I could tell he had not fully considered that he had the option to manage what information he was going to allow in. Years later, he still reminds me of that conversation and how many times the notion that HE is the one who has control over his mental filter has helped him stay focused and positive, instead of being derailed. Other people's negative energy will literally suck the life out of you and murder your dreams, if you let it.

A filter can function in two different ways. One model will support you; the other will hold you back. It is really important to tend to your filters to ensure that your personal filtering strategy is supporting you. In the first model, the one that will support you in your pursuits, you program your filters to let in what you want to pass through to you (positive attitudes, powerful examples of how others have created success) and block out the information and attitudes that you do not want (nay-sayers, other people's negative energy). In the second model, the one that will hold you back, you unintentionally block out what you DO want more of (thoughts that you are inherently unstoppable and capable of achieving whatever you put your mind to) and allow what you actually want less of (doubt, negative self-talk) to pass through.

Don't let yourself off the hook—because what's at stake is the quality of your future results. Examine your filters frequently. Mend them when they begin to fail and upgrade them when needed. As you examine them, look for anything that you have inadvertently allowed in, as well as what you have inadvertently allowed to get blocked out and trapped in those filters. If you can keep the bad seeds from landing in your garden in the first place, you won't have to pull weeds later.

Speak Only What You Want to Experience

Another pattern that breeds more and faster success is this: Speak only what you want to experience. Your words are the window into your beliefs. Your language has tremendous power, and your language patterns and choices are either supporting you or derailing you. The distance between you and anything that you want is in *your language*. In this case, language includes both your spoken words (external language) and your thoughts (internal language). Let's start by focusing on spoken words.

If you can buy into the idea that how we express ourselves—what we say and how we say it—has an impact on our thinking, and if you buy into this idea that our thoughts have a role in the results that we create, then you might see how the power of our words has a role in our outcomes. Our words are chosen and delivered from our conscious mind. Recent advancements in neuroscience have revealed that our subconscious mind is constantly monitoring and looking for guidance and commands coming to it from our conscious mind. The ultimate power of our subconscious mind is still to be determined; however, consensus among neuroscientists leads to the fact that much of our power to impact our future results and our ability to attract things and experiences into our lives resides not in our conscious mind, but in our subconscious mind.

Therefore, when you *speak only what you want to experience*, you are kicking into gear a Manifesting Trifecta, including the power of:

1. Your conscious mind
2. Your subconscious mind
3. The Law of Attraction

Focus Matters

Marie came to me with a desire to advance in her career, and specifically, to get picked for the next level executive management position that had recently become available in her firm. In one of her first sessions, I asked her to describe the situation, the competition for the position and her take on her areas of strength and weakness as it pertained to her ability to get the opportunity and to succeed in the new position. There were two sets of data that I was seeking in this part of our conversation. First, to get a feel for the "lay of the land" at her company as Marie saw it and secondly, I was watching for the words that she chose and which details she chose to share with me. Right out of the gate, Marie described her concern that she would probably not be taken seriously, that people still saw her as topped out in her position as a junior manager and that it was not likely that she would actually get the job. She continued, describing concerns that she had from times in her past in which she had not performed well, gone for a promotion and not gotten it, and how she mostly felt stressed out trying to keep everything together.

It was telling that when asked to describe the situation—competition for the position and her strengths and weaknesses—that her comments were entirely focused on her shortcomings and times when she had not succeeded. While it is really valuable to be aware of what we have going for us as well as what we may currently lack, you can learn a lot about a person by what they chose to talk about and highlight. Similarly, we can learn a lot about our own state of mind by being aware of our own choices in what we routinely lead with, or continually return to, in conversations, both external conversations with others and internal conversations with ourselves through our thoughts.

Left unchecked, with Marie's focus on her shortcomings, and based upon the notion that what we put our focus on expands, Marie was not likely to present herself in a way that would ultimately build the confidence in those interviewing her that would inspire and motivate them to pick her for the promotion.

It was time to bring Marie back to the idea of *speaking only what she wanted to experience*. In the following weeks, she practiced being much more conscious of what she chose to talk about. In both her thinking and in her conversations, she moved her focus from what she feared to what she wanted, from why she might fail to why she would succeed, to defining herself by her attributes and talents, not by her faults, doubts and shortcomings. Since some of our patterns of thought and behavior have been with us for years, we might not even be aware of these unconscious patterns as they have grown and anchored in us over time, little by little. Like so many other things, though, once we become aware of these patterns and the unnecessary harm they are creating, we can shatter them and build new, more beneficial ones.

So again, *speak only what you want to experience!*

Vent Mode

For those of you wondering how the hell anyone could possibly live up to this standard, let me add a very important distinction. It is absolutely OK, and in fact essential, to vent. It is OK to express your frustration or disappointment. The key is how, when and how frequently you are in vent mode. If you want to engage the power of your language, only stay in vent mode for a short period of time and be clear that you are in vent mode. We are human and we are not always going to be pumped about the way something turned out. Upset, disappointed, frustrated… that's all part of the deal. But we are Warriors defending our primary belief that we are connected, protected, guided and loved—and that setbacks are not indicators of anything except that we are learning and progressing toward success. This is hugely important.

The greatest military leaders throughout history were mere humans also. They absolutely had disappointments and setbacks, some of which resulted in the loss of the lives of many men and women under their command. You can bet that they had moments where they let their emotions out, yelled, cried and pondered their ability to lead. They vented. However, this is something that only a very few people were ever allowed to witness. Once the venting process was over, they knew that, for the well-being of their unit, they had to switch gears and focus on what to do from this moment forward. They embraced another powerful pattern—spending 5% of their available time, energy and resources focused on the problem, and 95% of their time, energy and resources focused on the solution. In fact, this is a big part of the Warrior Code, so let me repeat!

Warrior Code: Spend 5% of your time, energy and resources on the problem and 95% on the solution.

Considering that language has such power, it's easy to see how the words you choose actually direct your focus—and contribute to the quality of your outcomes. When you talk about how things aren't going well, how you're angry about this or that, how people are letting you down—or just complaining in general, you are reinforcing those negative outcomes in your mind, creating ever-deeper ruts in your brain. Then guess what, it shouldn't come as a surprise when it turns out that by using such words over and over you are actually attracting all those things that you don't want.

The same is true the other way around. If you are routinely talking about things in terms of how you want them to turn out, then that's what you'll attract. For example, which one of these statements is going to attract and reinforce a positive or negative outcome? "I am not good at this sport" or "Throw it to me, I'll catch that clutch pass!"

A few thoughts on how this same principle can help you in modifying your *internal* language, your thoughts: When it comes to engaging your Manifesting Trifecta (the power of your conscious mind, subconscious mind, and the Law of Attraction), there are only two differences between your spoken words and your thoughts.

1. Your spoken words connect with other people and create expectations for your success or failure in their minds.
2. You can choose your words, but not your thoughts.

The people that we interact with will make judgments about our ability to succeed based in part on how we express ourselves. We all do this. We can't help it. As we said earlier, your words are the windows into your beliefs. Think about the example above. Who are you most frequently going to throw the ball to? The person that says, "I am not good at this sport" or "Throw it to me, I'll catch that clutch pass!" Yep!

The same is true in any aspect of life. It is impossible to activate an "I won't be denied, we will succeed" attitude while simultaneously using words like, "Sure hope we don't screw up" or "I never do very well in these situations."

Warrior Code: You are going to have an attitude anyway, you might as well make it an extraordinary one!

Thoughts Happen!

By conditioning ourselves, we can absolutely take control of our *spoken* word choices and increase our power as a result. *Thoughts*, on the other hand, are trickier because they just show up. Check this out. Try really hard right now <u>not</u> to envision in your mind's eye a red Ferrari. Hmmm… were you successful in NOT seeing a red Ferrari? If you were, please call me because I want to know how you did that. More than likely, you ended up with a red Ferrari in your thoughts. So what is that all about? The instruction was to NOT envision a red Ferrari. That's what I mean about control of our thoughts being more difficult.

While we can be deliberate in our choice of words, we are all going to have thoughts that we would rather not have. Thoughts of doubt, thoughts of fear, thoughts of failing, thoughts of dreams crashing and burning. We are all going to experience fear storms. So, what is the Warrior's Code when it comes to our thoughts? *Don't fight them!* Fighting them is like trying to fight the sun coming up in the morning. Disempowering thoughts, just like the sun's rise into the sky, are going to happen. The key is to allow them (because frankly, you can't do a damn thing about their showing up, anyway) but not validate or accept them. While you really can't simply choose *not* to have disempowering thoughts, you can absolutely right size them, recognize that they are coming to you from your ego, and then move forward anyway.

Warrior Code: Don't fight fear.
Instead, acknowledge that fear is present,
smile and move forward with grace.

Never forget that you are a Warrior on the path to success! You can build and keep unstoppable momentum by launching every day with a check-in with what is already aligned for success and what needs to be adjusted. Just like a chiropractor adjusts your spine, you have the ability and the responsibility to adjust your attitude, strength, expectations and your physical, emotional, intellectual, and even spiritual body.

Warrior Commandment # 4: Attitude and Positive Expectation

Positive expectation has a relationship to an optimistic attitude but is not the *same* as an optimistic attitude. There have been numerous studies regarding the effects of optimism on job performance. Sales people, for instance, who were more optimistic have been shown to have better sales results than those who were pessimistic. This is in line with the "Expectancy Theory" first developed in 1964 by Yale University professor Victor Vroom (no pun intended with that last name!). Professor Vroom's is a motivational theory based on cognitive psychology. It stipulates that people are more motivated by their own conscious expectations of what will happen if they do certain things—and are more successful and productive when they believe those expectations will be realized.

Obviously, this is linked to optimism, but it's a little bit different. Optimism is very, very important and valuable to have. Positive expectancy, however, is the ability to look at each situation and each segment of your day with the expectation that is it going to go well, that things are going to go the way you want them to… *or better*. It is the habit of approaching everything with the mindset that you EXPECT that what you have in mind—*or something even better*—will arise. It is an acceptance that even if something doesn't go the way you intended it to, it ended up going the way that it was truly *supposed* to—and that it opened up even more doors and opportunities for you.

There's no question, people who adopt a core belief of positive expectancy experience more success. A friend and one time boss of mine, Michael, is an excellent example of the power of positive expectancy. Michael routinely, in his heart, believes that things are going to go well.

Even when setbacks occur, he immediately shifts gears and looks for how to go to the next level and make whatever is next amazing. He created a lot of success in his life because he embodied positive expectancy and because he was also phenomenally resilient. At one point in his career when he was fired from the company that he was with for twenty years, he took that hit in stride and immediately began plans to build a new company that was even better than the previous one.

The combination of high energy, focus and positive expectation creates the foundation for getting more of what you want and delivering more of what you've got.

EXERCISE FOR CHECKING YOUR POSITIVE EXPECTATION LEVEL
Make a habit of using these internal check-ins to be sure you're focused and totally game-on. They will help you get the most from each segment of your day, as well as killer results over time.

Prior to every meeting, appointment, or part of your day, quickly check in with yourself to make sure you are bringing your best. Give yourself a score in each of the areas listed below.

A 10 indicates "Couldn't possibly be better" and a 1 indicates "Lower than low". You'll quickly see where you need to power up!

My Energy level (1 to 10)

My level of Focus (1 to 10)

My level of Positive Expectation (1 to 10)

Let's look at a concrete example of how having an expectation that things are going to go your way can be beneficial. We have a rental house in Colorado. When the lease was up and the family that had been renting the house decided to move out, they called me and said, "Hey, we're not going to be able to pay the last month's rent; you'll have to use our security deposit for this month's rent." I immediately thought, "Well, that ain't great because that leaves me with a lot of financial exposure." When I mentioned the situation to friends, they universally responded with, "Will, you've got to evict this guy and get him out of there."

But my thought was, "You know, I don't think that I do." Instead, I decided to give the renters a positive reputation to live up to. I called the man back and told him that my experience of him was that he always showed up as a man of honor—and that I knew he would do the right thing. Everyone thought I was crazy and repeated their call, "Matthews, you've got to get this guy out of there now!" I decided, however, to stay with my idea and my expectation that he was going to pull through for me. And when I did, it turned out that when he moved, he left the house in great condition.

As mentioned previously, I believe that if you have faith that people are going to pull through for you—or if you believe they won't—your belief will play a role in whether they do the right thing or not. Some of the friends that were in the place of, "Oh no, Will, you've got to evict him or he is going to screw you over" probably would have had that kind of quality experience if they had been in my shoes and decided to move forward on the eviction track.

In my conversation with a speaker friend of mine recently, I was relaying the story of my experience with my renter—the whole piece about the effect of positive expectation and how it ended up being great, I never had to serve legal papers on anybody, and I got a better outcome than I would have if I had chosen the negative expectancy/protect myself route. I could see a light bulb go on for him. He then told me his story about the local cable company that had let him down five times consecutively. Five different commitments as to when they would be at his house to install his Internet connection, and five no-shows. *Five* of them! He was freaking out. Hearing my story, he asked, "Are you saying that you think my expectation that things with the cable company were going to continue to go poorly had a role in my having a frustrating and negative experience?"

And I said, "I do! The cool thing is that there is no downside to deciding to embrace the idea that positive expectancy can produce a better result, to see if it turns things around for you. You can give it a try—just as an experiment—to see if it helps make your life easier and if it brings you more of the results you want."

He answered, "It's hard for me to do that because of my history with them."

And I said, "I get it. But there is no downside to this! Just consider the idea that you have a role, through the law of attraction—or whatever you prefer to call it—that when you expect someone to pull through for you, you create an effect on that outcome. Likewise, if you expect someone to *not* pull through for you, to let you down, to disappoint you, you will have a similar experience—only on the negative side.

Remember the story of Steve outlined earlier in the book where he was so frustrated and stated, "Why can't I just have a bunch of robots that do exactly what I need them to do and work as hard as I do? I can't stand it anymore. I'd fire everybody but I would just end up with a new group creating the same problems. Why would I want to do that?" Steve and I worked hard on shifting his energy to create a foundation of positive expectation, and he turned his situation around.

Check in with yourself. Where are you making things more difficult by harboring a core expectation that the people in your personal or professional lives are going to disappoint you and not pull through?

Warrior Code: Positive Expectation
is the precursor to Positive Results

Warrior Commandment # 5: The Immense Power of Personal Leverage

Endurance comes from finding strength when times get hard. Strength is often created by staying connected to the reason WHY you have committed to a particular goal or outcome. Learning how to keep leverage on yourself, especially during dips in your level of passion, energy and determination, more often than not, will make the difference between success and failure. Here's how leverage works.

While all change happens in an instant, change only happens when the right amount of leverage is applied. It takes energy to implement change, while it is so easy to simply stay on the course that you are already on. That is why some people are in careers or relationships or poor physical condition even though they are constantly talking about wanting to make a change. They will only actually make the change when they foresee massive pain to staying on the course—or massive pleasure in making the shift to a new course. Just like them, you will ONLY make a change in your life when you have enough leverage to make staying on the familiar course and sustaining the status quo no longer an option.

When stagnating in growing your business or reaching any other big goal, you may need to create new levels of leverage in order to reestablish or increase your momentum. You may have terrific goals but check in to see if they exist in the realm of "I should…" or in the realm of "I must…" As a test, ask yourself, "What would I do if I didn't reach that goal?" If your response is not tied back to heartfelt emotion, such as, "Oh my God, if I didn't achieve this I would want to crawl in a hole and hide," then your goal is merely a "should" or "it would be nice to have." Attainment of your goal is hindered because your "Why" is impotent. Your goal lacks sufficient leverage.

If that is the case, you NEED leverage—and you need it NOW! Leverage is the thing that applies the right kind of pressure on you and creates emotion. Emotion creates motion and fires up action on your part. If there is no real pain associated with not reaching your goal, emotion has no power to motivate you, to push you to take action.

Leverage is most effective when it is directly tied to an emotional response. Let's explore a few examples of how leverage has helped me and others reach goals that we had been unable to achieve in the past.

Jack's Motivator

I once worked with a truly outstanding man named Jack who, although really successful in his career in the entertainment industry, had a deep desire to break into the public speaking business. He was hugely passionate and had a message that he was driven to share with people. While I had known him to be an absolute go-getter in so many aspects of his career and life, he was dragging his feet when it came to getting in front of people and organizations and pitching his speaking offerings. During our coaching sessions he would commit to reach out to ten or fifteen companies to pitch his topic and presentation, but when I checked in with him at the start of the next session to see if he had fulfilled his commitment, he would have to admit that he hadn't. Instead of reaching out to ten or fifteen companies, he would have maybe called two.

This was so unlike him and, because of that, I knew that there was something underneath this that was creating the hesitation and lack of results. Turns out that while he was really good at raising funds and selling projects as a representative of the entertainment company that he worked for, selling himself to companies felt different and was very intimidating. It was breakthrough time—time for some leverage to help him take more meaningful steps in the direction of his dreams.

I said, "All right, the path that you are on is not going to get you the result that I know you want. Let's step it up and get some real leverage on you. You have stated that in order to get your speaking business launched you need to connect with ten to fifteen companies every week. Do you still see this as a critical component to your success?"

"Yes, absolutely," he said.

"OK, then let's make this real. Your commitment is to connect with ten to fifteen companies each week for the next eight weeks. What is the "juice" on this if you do not make that commitment happen in any given week?"

He knew what I meant by "juice". It's the painful thing that he would have to do if he did not pull through. He thought for a minute and said, "OK, I've got it. Will, if in any given week, I do not connect with ten or more companies, then I will write a check to your favorite charity for $100." Hmmm... not bad. That would certainly apply some leverage from the financial side of things. The only problem was that this was definitely not juicy enough to move his commitment from a "should" or "nice-to-have" to an absolute "must". Besides, writing a check to a charity also has a "feel-good" component to it.

"Nah", I said. "Let's crank this up a few levels in a couple of different ways so that there is no way that you would ever not reach your weekly commitment. Rather than a $100 check to my favorite charity, let's make it a $1,000 check written to a white supremacy organization." I knew that the idea of writing a $1,000 check to a group like that would be so outrageous and so painful that he would do ANYTHING to make sure that that writing that check would NEVER happen, including fulfilling his commitment to pitch his topic to ten or more companies each week.

You see, Jack is a man with a deep commitment to racial equality. This was precisely the level of pain, or more accurately the *avoidance* of pain, that would surely create the leverage he needed to do whatever it took. Needless to say, Jack met his goal... and then some in part due to having massive leverage. He now speaks many times each year, adding a new stream of income and giving him a creative outlet that he loves.

Sometimes leverage gives us what we need in order to reach in as deeply as necessary to fulfill our commitments—which will then lead us to our desired goals and outcomes.

My clients are not the only ones who need to apply leverage to reach their goals, however.

Several years ago, I needed to finish my business plan... and I was procrastinating. The plan was really important because at the time, I thought that I was going to need to attract some investment capital and the business plan was a critical step on that path. I kept putting it off because—well, have you ever noticed that we knock out projects that are relatively inconsequential with ease because we haven't tied our identity to them? Those projects that really move us out into the spotlight and add new levels of exposure are the ones that we'll procrastinate on and put off because completing them moves us more closely to the point of no return.

As long as we are just talking about writing a plan to attract investors, we are excited and also quite safe. After all, we can talk, and often do, about what we are going to do. But once the plan is finished and sent out, that is where the rubber meets the road. In the moments that follow, we are massively vulnerable and our plan will either succeed or fail—and so, we think, shall WE succeed or fail. Lots of identity attached = lots of potential to procrastinate.

Long story, short: I finally got some leverage on myself. I committed and declared that I would not shower or bathe until I had completed the business plan. And I didn't. I even attended a board meeting in the midst of all this. Thankfully, I don't think anyone noticed anything askew—or at least they were kind enough to pretend not to! Two days later, my business plan was completed. Got to admit that that next shower felt amazing.

A second example: When I was in the process of recording my first product, the same delays occurred for the very same reason. As long as my new audio program was "yet to come," I was in the safety of "potential". As soon as it went to market, I was exposed and my identity—the way I defined myself and how others would see me—was fully at stake. So again, I finally had had enough of my procrastination and declared that I would not work out until I had completed the recording. By the way, anyone who knows me well, knows how much I value my workouts and the alignment that they provide to me physically, mentally, emotionally and spiritually. Again, and needless to say—the leverage worked and I am so proud of the audio program that I created, *Expanding the Glimpse, Daily Tools for Creating the Life and Business of Your Dreams,* which has sold thousands of copies since its release.

Warrior Code: You can make anything happen if you have enough leverage on yourself.

Warrior Commandment # 6: Rethink Your Rules—Comfort Zone Be Damned

"I don't know if I am entering my comfort zone or not. I've never been there."

—John Matthews

All the zest of life exists outside your comfort zone. In fact, risk is the real fountain of youth as taking risks keeps us young. Don't get me wrong… I know that the mere mention of taking risks can bring our fears up to the surface and can feel very scary. But in a very real way, the *real* risk is in never letting go of that fear and never stepping into the unknown with a sense of confidence, trust and positive expectation.

Don't wait for the perfect time to take a big, big step toward your dreams. There is no such thing as the perfect time. The perfect time will simply never arrive. We are called to go all in... right now!

Your outside world and the results that you create are an expression of your internal beliefs and expectations, your willingness to truly venture forward into what might seem risky when you sense in your heart that the move is right. Remember that you are not here to be typical. Be more committed to your goal than anyone else, period.

<u>Warrior Commandment # 7</u>: Build Your Power-Boosting Environments

Creating quality. Inside the cover of a Rolex watch, all the pieces are highly engineered, manufactured and polished with incredible precision. Every Rolex is made to perform exquisitely well. As amazing as the Rolex is, it is equally important that the watch, once made, exists in an environment that will support its sustained excellence. Usually, it's well cared-for (after all, they cost a lot!) and not allowed to be subject to damage—at least not deliberately. But if a Rolex winds up in a trash-masher or a garbage grinder, it doesn't really matter how well it was made or what precision and skill went into its construction, it will never again perform the way that it was meant to perform. The same is true for each of us. We are made to succeed, but it is up to us to assume responsibility for the environment, both internal and external—in which we exist and operate.

As we have discussed, much of success is an internal game, but it is also critical that you are very particular as you fashion the external environment in which you operate day in and day out. The effect of your environment in supporting, sustaining, and accelerating your success cannot be overlooked. The bottom line is that you live, move and build your future with a mix of internal and external forces. The key is to be meticulous in the environment that you create for yourself because leaving this to chance is dangerous and foolish.

Self-empowerment is not an exclusively cerebral game. There are things you can do in your physical environment to empower yourself. Consider these:

- What music gets you excited and pumped up? Get those songs on your playlist.
- What kind of visuals help you feel empowered and strong?
- Does exercise make you feel stronger and more energetic?
- Who in your inner circle of friends inspires you and brings out the best in you?

It's up to you to consciously, deliberately—with every move you make—set yourself up to win. So, pay attention to the environment you're creating in every moment, in every situation and deliberately create that environment for yourself. Be sure what you create jazzes you, inspires you, keeps you thinking big!

Identify and spend time in the presence of things that trigger you to think big. Let's make this point actionable right now.

Think of 10 songs that always inspire you or take you back in time to a moment when you felt incredibly proud or connected or happy. Start your list here, or if you would rather, just set up a new playlist with a title like "My Power Music". You can always add/delete/upgrade later. Do not go to the next chapter until you have your top ten in place—and be sure you include the songs that bring out the "unstoppableness" in you!

1.)

2.)

3.)

4.)

5.)

6.)

7.)

8.)

9.)

10.)

Now, look around your office or work area. After months or years of entering the same environment over and over, our awareness of the things in that environment and the effect those things have on us is often reduced. While we aren't overly conscious of those things that we have seen on our walls for months or years, they are likely either inspiring or uninspiring, power-building or power-draining.

If the latter is true, time to do some remodeling. This remodeling doesn't need to be expensive. Add a plant, a poster of one of your favorite sports or hobbies, some quotes from your favorite authors, photographs from your favorite vacation, a crayon drawing from your second-grader—anything that moves you and makes you smile.

Remember that life can only be lived one day at a time... and today is a brand new day, a brand new opportunity. So, bring in more color, more sound, more memories that can keep you focused on the possibilities.

Warrior Commandment # 8—Ignite Your Super Powers

What is your "Super Power"? Tony Hsieh, CEO of the phenomenal online shoe and clothing company Zappos, exposed me to the idea of Super Powers. They are the skills that you and others recognize as huge assets for you—those particular skills or sets of skills that you bring to the team, to your business, to your family, to the table, to the planet. Too often, we are keenly capable of identifying our weak spots, deficiencies and challenges, but not so talented at identifying those attributes and strengths that set us apart in our ability to contribute, deliver and provide value. Even the Super Heroes we know so well from comic books and Hollywood movies struggle with their own unique challenges, at the same time that they employ their extraordinary Super Powers in the pursuit of good.

What are you Super Powers?
What would need to be included on a poster created to highlight your super abilities, attributes and skills?

What strengths do you bring to your business, teams, family, relationships, friendships and community? Identify and acknowledge your Super Powers. Doing so is probably long overdue.

Bringing your best and tapping into your Super Powers is one way to start showing up more authentically. After all, what's the point if you can't truly be yourself? And just as importantly, who can make "bringing your true and authentic self" happen? That's right, no one but *you*.

When you allow yourself to step into the pure flow of who you are and let the façade finally and forever fall to the ground, you will look back and wonder, *why did I hold up that false picture of myself for so long?*

What do you have to lose by being yourself?
What do you have to gain?

To consistently access and deliver what you have to offer demands that you are truthful in your interactions with yourself and with other people. It requires that you set a standard of being truthful *always*. The only alternative to not being truthful is lying. The biggest problem with lying is that lying only postpones the inevitable. The problem doesn't permanently go away when we lie—in fact, it usually amplifies.

It is similar to the concept of deferred maintenance on a house. You can recognize problems with your house and fix things as they break or decide, instead, to let it slide and fix it later. Being untruthful with yourself or others is taking the "fix it later" option. While that "I'll push it off until later" might sound good at the time, it leads inevitably to greater problems down the road. If you are not being truthful with other people then you are making the decision to have inauthentic and therefore, weak relationships.

Authenticity

Being authentic is not always easy, but it is a critical component to the success of the Warrior. We are challenged frequently to give up our authenticity to fit in or to get along. Your ability to respond effectively is in direct proportion to your sense of knowing where you stand, what you are committed to and where you are going. If you don't know what you stand for, then you stand for the status quo—you stand for your life and your experience just as it is right now. Ask yourself what you are doing today to stand in support of your vision for your life.

You are not here to fit in, but rather to stand out, to express your unique gifts. Every time you choose to muffle your true voice, your true message, and instead settle for fitting in, you are cheating yourself and those around you.

Don't keep looking for yourself where you are not. Don't keep looking for yourself where you used to be. Instead, connect more deeply to your inner guidance.

You and I are wired from the factory to have fun, laugh, take risks and be passionate. And the way you display passion doesn't have to be the same way that I do, or the same way anyone else does. It is important, however, to open the channel to your passion, because it's a crucial part of being yourself. It's also important to project that passion to others. Believe it or not, people will feel increasingly comfortable letting you in, the more genuinely "you" you are.

How you show up in the eyes of others is a bit like a movie projector. The quality of the picture that's projected to the world (that is, the picture of our genuine selves) is only as good as the film running in our projectors. Whatever is on that film is amplified, magnified, and brought to the outside, to the "screen". There are no two ways about it. You're projecting what's inside, outside. If there is incongruency or inauthenticity, everyone picks up on that. Because ultimately, how you show up "on screen" is how you show up in life. It's how others will experience you, know and think of you.

If the quality of our film is lousy, there's nothing we can do to mask that when it's projected on the screen. But if our film quality is high, the picture everyone sees will be crisp, clear, and fun to watch. How, then, can we ensure that the film we're running is of the highest quality?

I think you'll find that when you commit to project who you truly are into the world, and project from your core, your energy will go through the roof. You'll recapture all the energy it used to take just to hold up the façade of your less authentic self and you'll put it to better use. Holding up a façade is like trying to lean in and support a falling brick wall by yourself. It's a 24-hour-a-day operation, and it's draining.

What frees us is letting go of the notion that we need to be like someone else.

What and who are you pretending to be?

Showing up in your authentic self is the only way to unleash your Super Powers. When it comes to selling, promoting, attracting ideal clients—or even an ideal mate—nothing can replace the power of being authentic. When you project from that genuine place, others will admire you for it, and even fall in love with you. Why? Because they're detecting something in you that they want for themselves—a kind of freedom and transparency no one can have while trying to be somebody else. You'll be amazed at how the universe responds to your authenticity, and how many people will step forward to accept and support you.

The world is crying out for more authenticity. Humans are not designed from a cookie-cutter mold. You don't have to fit into the shape that others want for you. So, let the mask fall to the floor, right now and forever. It's time to stop looking for yourself where you are not. Your only job is to be yourself.

> "Fitting in is boring for anyone that wants to be extraordinary"
> —Adam Levine

Stop watching every word you say. Be who you are! Let your quirkiness and creativity show. Don't dilute yourself by stifling your spirit, your spark. Because the BIG POINT here is that when you finally get tired of being who "they" want you to be, you'll find out who you really are.

True authenticity includes recognizing patterns so you can change the outdated ones—that is, the patterns that may be comfortable, but aren't working for you. It also involves discovering principles and building habits that *do* work for you. That means being honest with yourself, your team, your family, your clients. Be willing to see things as they are and be *intentional* in your dealings with others. Embrace and really inhabit the changes you need to make. Start by opening your heart and allowing your spirit to radiate through you.

Now, some words of caution.

First, becoming more authentically "you" can be scary, but it's not as scary as that Halloween mask you've been wearing, and not as suffocating. Have faith in yourself, remembering that if you don't, you'll continually seek the approval of other people, thereby diluting your authentic voice and threatening your dreams.

With that said, authenticity is really fairly simple. Authenticity is simply having congruency of your identity, beliefs and actions. Authentic leaders succeed when others don't primarily because the high level of alignment that they have keeps them from carrying the heavy load of holding up ridiculous facades. If you want to reduce stress and tension in your life, reach in and bring your authentic self to the surface.

Your only job is to be yourself, so be bold and cross some lines—say what you need to say. Say it out loud! Be real, be your authentic self. What do you stand for?

Warrior Code: Super Powers arise only when you are being authentic and true to yourself.

Warrior Commandment # 9—Courage, Wisdom and Your Connection to Your Heart

Your heart will take you to amazing places that your mind won't let you go. Look inside yourself for guidance and direction. Everything you need in order to accomplish your goals exists within you already—it just requires your acknowledgement—and your action.

"Why do we have to listen to our hearts?" the boy asked when they made camp that day. "Because, wherever you find your heart, that is where you'll find your treasure."
—Paulo Coelho, The Alchemist

Listen to Your Heart

Listen for your wake-up calls. They are all around you. You're here to learn a very unique set of lessons. When you learn them, you can move forward. But until you do, you'll remain in a loop in which the same lessons show up again and again. When you listen to your intuition and take a different course, whatever has been haunting you or holding you back will simply disappear. I know it may sound hard to believe, but it's the way the universe works.

You have great instincts. They have just been buried under a heavy coating of tribal thinking, a little self-doubt and years of neglect. Learn to listen to your body, that little voice inside your head, the "telling" feeling in your gut. Nobody, no matter how wise, is more wise than your own instincts. If it doesn't feel right, don't do it.

Listening begins with creating space in our lives—and creating space breeds creativity. We can make space by first making a commitment to coming "home to ourselves" every day. But what does "coming home to ourselves" mean? It's simple. Spend some time alone. Shut down the transmitter, as well as the receiver. Meditate. You have the right to remain silent! So take advantage of some quiet time.

The Encounter at the Airport

Recently, while I was in the Denver airport on the way to catch a flight, an older gentleman who spoke with a heavy accent asked me how to get to his gate. I looked at his ticket and noted that our gates were right next to each other, so I offered to walk with him. He was "on holiday," as he put it. He had traveled to the United States from his home in India.

I mentioned that I'd always wanted to visit India and asked him about the differences he'd experienced in his interactions with people in the United States compared to those that he had with people in India. He said the two countries were, "really totally different. In India when we have something important that we are trying to resolve, we connect to our heart for the answer." He put his hands over his heart. "Here in the U.S., most people seem to trust this," and he pointed to his head, as he searched for the word that he wanted.

"The mind," I said, filling in the English for him.

"Yes, the mind," he answered. "Much too hard on you, too much stress, too hard on the body—and most of the answers aren't found there. Connect to your heart for the answers to all of your life's questions. It is there that you will find them. It is in your heart that your wisdom lives."

As we arrived at our gates, I studied his face and stature. "Peaceful" was the best word to describe him. He was off to Philadelphia and I to Salt Lake City. I wished him safe travels and we parted ways, and as I walked away, I looked back at him. I suddenly recognized that our meeting was not just a chance meeting; rather, he had given me a gift that I'd forgotten. He had touched my life.

He reminded me how imperative it is to stay connected to your core, to listen to your heart, and to lead with your heart. You know that expression, "You must be out of your mind?" Well, let's hope so! Instead, be in your heart. Think of it this way: When someone is sharing life's last moments with a person they love, what is often expressed? Not, "You'll live on in my head forever." But rather, "You will live on in my heart forever."

When you identify first from your heart, then your head, you will understand something new that you didn't understand before.

Change/connection/rapport occurs when there is a shift in the heart of a person. Lead with your heart, physically, as in your posture when entering a room—and also figuratively as you lead others first and foremost from your heart.

Never forget that there is an essence, a *you* that resides within you that is true and unchanged by the events and conditions and experiences of this life. It's always there, always ready for you to return to it, to step back into it—so come back home to yourself frequently.

When listening and acting from your heart and intuition, some powerful things come into play. There's a very definite advantage available to you when you build the habit of "heart first, head second". True Warriors know to first seek guidance from their heart before taking action.

An Exercise for Getting Back on Track

When you feel like you're freaking out, losing your grip or standing on shaky ground, take a minute to check in on yourself through this simple exercise. In any moment you can check to see where your energy is focused and where you are placing your attention.

While standing comfortably, close your eyes and just do your best to relax for a minute. Become aware of where you feel the most energy in your body. If you don't feel any energy right away, that's OK, just relax a little more and become just a little more aware of your breathing— breathing in and breathing out. Start to become aware of the energy (or perhaps tension) and where it is emanating from you. Is this density of energy coming primarily from your head area, stomach area... elsewhere?

Wherever the most noticeable energy or tension is located, whether it is existing in your head or near your stomach or anywhere else, imagine allowing that energy to gently leave your body and move straight forward just 6" or 7" in front of the area in your body where you have sensed it.

Now, when you are ready, allow this ball of energy to move slowly either up or down to the area directly in front of your heart. Then allow the energy from your heart to reach out and connect to the energy that you have placed there in front of your heart.

Ask your heart for guidance. Ask your heart for the answers. Simply relax and listen until you have opened to hearing those answers. Trust that they will come.

Next, open your eyes and smile—and be grateful for the gift of those answers.

Now, move forward in the direction that your heart's guidance provided to you.

Warrior Code: Wisdom comes from connection to heart first, then head.

Any time that you need answers, guidance or peace, you can always come home to your heart. We've all been conditioned to look outside ourselves for answers. But the answers we need, the ones that are right for us, are inside—it's just a matter of listening for them. The answers to your questions, big and small, are always with you, always available, always in your heart just waiting for you to ask for them.

Another Personal Story

Several years ago, when I was attending a meeting of the National Speakers Association, I interviewed several well-known speakers for a radio show that I hosted at that time. As I did this, the growing feeling that I was an outsider began to creep into my thinking (Hello Ego Gremlins!). This was not brought on by anything anyone else said;

rather, I just slowly began to allow these negative thoughts to dominate my thinking. The more that I stayed in the sense that I was separate, not part of the group, but outside looking in, the more I began to seize up. My breathing became shallow and I felt that I was about to have a panic attack. Suddenly, there was a part of me that wanted to cancel the rest of the interviews and just get the hell out of there.

I realized what was happening to me, but it was tough to tackle it and turn it around. I knew I had to do something to address and change my mental state, though. As soon as I could, I left the interview room and found a place in the courtyard where I could be alone and figure out how to manage this. I grabbed a pen and note pad and wrote the following words without really even being fully conscious of what I was writing.

- I am connected, protected, guided and loved.
- I now reconnect to the common thread that connects my heart to all hearts.
- The white light that surrounds me now washes away the pain of any rejection and clears the path of all ugly, limiting thoughts.
- Each man is my brother, each woman is my sister, and our souls are connected in a deep way that even I don't completely understand.
- I treasure each experience and I value and honor each person, for their pain is my pain and their joy is my joy.
- I now move out of the darkness of despair and re-enter the beautiful, warm, healing white light.
- My head is now clear of concern and doubt and pain—and I am refreshed and re-energized as I push through to joy, gratitude, and connectedness.
- I now exude love, compassion and peace from every cell in my body and being.

- My mission is clear and any challenges will be met and overcome as I gain momentum and find my path through the woods.
- I conquer all setbacks with increased determination and trust.
- I fully trust and peacefully let go.

With my perspective realigned, I re-entered the interview room and felt an amazing connection with each person that came to meet with me. The resulting interviews were some of the best in the entire span of years that the radio show existed!

What I have just described is a fear-processing method, a very effective one. As you can see, it is simple—it involves turning your mind around by focusing on what is true, what is positive, what is good. And then acting upon it. Ask yourself what support systems, both internal and external, you can put into place now to keep yourself focused and moving forward when the fear storms or insecurity hit.

The key is to start to manage your state of mind. Connect yourself to what's real, not to your fears, and not to fear's illusions. When you feel insignificant, separate or alone, change your state by saying:

"I am connected, protected, guided and loved and I now reconnect to the common thread that connects my heart to all hearts."

When moving in this sense of peace, power, and wisdom, you will find that the ground beneath any limiting beliefs will begin to crumble.

By learning to do this, you will not only rescue yourself, but as you are an example for others around you, you will also inspire others to move through their day, including the great days as well as the tough days from a strong foundation of connectedness, significance, trust and peace.

Warrior Commandment # 10—Abolishing Fear Storms

One of the great benefits of getting out of our heads and into our hearts is that it gives us the context to right-size fear and its role in our lives. From the heart-based foundation of knowing that you are connected, protected, guided and loved, more and more opens up and becomes available for you. It is almost impossible to embrace the idea that we are connected, protected, guided and loved—and simultaneously embrace that we are standing on dangerous ground and that we are going to fail, crash and burn.

While that is true, guess what typically derails a genuine, heart-generated vision of your ultra compelling future? Those darn fear storms rolling in and blocking your view, that's what. Fear is created by our egos. Its sole mission is to keep us from stepping up to a bigger, better experience by throwing in doubt, worries, comparisons, and concerns about stepping out of what is "certain" into the batter of your beautiful new cake.

Isn't it strange that the primary force that holds us back and keeps us thinking small (if we let it) is not an external force, but an internal one? It's something we create—and the important thing to realize is that because of that, it is also under our control.

So, what to do when fear strikes? Challenge every limiting, negative, fearful belief that arises in your thoughts. When you hear an old fear-based file running, and some of these have been onboard influencing your view of what is possible for you for a LONG time, get all "Warrior" with it and immediately hit the "STOP" button. No more being the victim of your fear thoughts.

Right in the moment that you become aware of fear stepping in, question. Question where that thought is coming from—is it a legitimate message from your intuition cluing you in on something to be aware of or is it just chatter from your freaked-out ego screaming for attention and engaging in unfounded scare tactics?

No more responding as a victim and no more being at the whim of these ridiculous ego scare tactics. Unless you surrender your appropriate self-leadership position, you are in charge, not your ego. These thoughts of fear and trepidation are simply rolled out in front of you. They are testing you and your resolve. They are waiting for you to expose them as the old, tired beliefs that they are.

A worn out, false belief is waiting for you to *expose it* so you can *dispose of it*!

Warrior Code: "There are NO victims, only volunteers."
—Robert Anthony

Reality check: Any chance that you are using one or more of your "fears" as a crutch, something that you have become kind of comfortable with? After all, moving forward without an attachment to fear means that you have fewer and fewer excuses to anchor back to. Moving forward without fear means that you are solely responsible for your success or failure? Scary? Not when you really think about it. Isn't it the absolute most empowering idea ever that YOU are the determining factor, with full ownership of your success or failure?

With practice, you can eliminate unnecessary fear from your life, and when you do, you'll experience an amazing boost in performance and a relaxed confidence.

When you are able to return to your core, to your truth, you come to understand that the most powerful, miracle-minded thing to do is not to deny your fear, but to see it as an assignment to learn and grow.

Fear is what will lead you to feeling small, separate, and disconnected. In fearful states, we tend to feel separate from people who have the things we want. The chasm you build through your belief in separateness widens and deepens and becomes difficult to cross—that is, until you develop a mentality of being connected.

We are all just individual expressions of the same spirit. That's what's real. We know that we're all connected, and each of us has a choice about whether to go through life more peacefully and lovingly, or by polluting the world with more fear. In other words, what we choose to do individually can truly transform the world. *How awesome is that?*

There's an opportunity cost to showing up fearfully. Yes, when in a fearful state of mind, our emotional and psychological fortresses take a hit. But even more important, is the cost to you in productivity. The time that's required to struggle with fear and insecurity could be spent more effectively—with the result being a stronger, smarter, more successful you. And how about happier? What's the price tag for that? Feeling anxious or afraid is a luxury we can't afford, though one we often indulge in anyway. Our fears are what keep us in the dark.

What fears and stories are you blowing up in your head right now? You know what to do!

ACTIONABLE STEPS FOR BEING A STRONG WARRIOR

Warriors take charge of their futures. Your life from today forward is awaiting your command. Imagine that you have a clean, blank sheet of paper in front of you right now and your job is to describe the way you want your future to be. No references to the past or to the present, no historical challenges. Can you imagine what would be included in that list and description?

Action Step # 1:

Identify a time that you can devote to this and at that time, pull out a fresh sheet of paper (actually, the bigger the paper, the better—easel-size rocks!) and start writing the description of your desired future. What are the kinds of things that you want to make sure to include? What are the details of the future if you could make it just the way you want it? What would you like to attract into your life? What goals will drive you in this desired future?

When it comes to being brave, bold and courageous, never forget that everything that you seek to be, *you already are!*

Some questions to get you thinking:

1. What is your personal definition of success?
2. What attributes, qualities, traits, habits and patterns do you want to take forward into this next stage of your life?
3. What are you ready to let go of?
4. What are your non-negotiables? What do you stand for and what will you no longer tolerate?
5. What is the price you are willing to pay to stay within your comfort zone?
6. Who are your "Make It Happen People"? Who are the people that you can count on to hold you to a higher mission and vision for your life?
7. What do you love about what you are doing now?
8. What do you hate about what you are doing now?
9. What are you saying "Yes" to that you should be saying "No" to?
10. What are you saying "No" to that you should be saying "Yes" to?
11. What should you start doing, stop doing, and continue doing?
12. What are your top 5 values?
13. What are you doing when you feel most authentic? Most in ease and flow?
14. What are you doing when you are your "best" self?
15. Who are you becoming?

16. What is your secret wish? What would *you* most like to do with your time?

17. What are the contributions that you most want to make?

18. When do you feel most grounded? (spiritually, mentally, emotionally, physically, intellectually)

19. What would you change if you could?

20. What door are you being asked to open next?

21. What do you still need to clean up?

22. In what areas of your life are you settling?

Action Step # 2:

Organize your list into:

1. Commitments to new ways of executing, delivering, enjoying
2. Listing the things that you commit to no longer do
3. Top 5 guiding values
4. Top 5 near term-goals
5. Your "Make It Happen People" list

Action Step # 3:

Contact the people on your "Make It Happen People" list.

1. Let them know that you included them on the list.
2. Tell them why you included them, what you admire about them.
3. If they are someone that you want as a mentor, ask them if they would be willing to spend some time with you from time to time with a specific agenda for each meeting and total number of meetings.
4. Offer to make the same commitment to them if they are interested.

5. I want to be part of your team. Send me your answers to the questions above. Send them to <u>will@mpgcoaching.com</u> and I will respond with my thoughts about how to accelerate your success. Also, tell me where you are from and what you are committed to creating in your life.

Chapter 4

Master Resiliency

"A smooth sea never made a skilled mariner."
—English Proverb

Challenges, trials and setbacks are all part of the experience of a full life. To achieve and accomplish what you set out to do, you will need to stretch, reach, attempt... and yes, FAIL. Failing is not a bad thing. Although it usually feels bad in the moment, failure is a natural and essential part of your journey and growth. Here's the problem: So many times people respond to failure, setbacks or disappointments by shrinking back. Sometimes they shrink back forever from the part of their life in which they had the setback, choosing to avoid what they have identified as pain. They hope to sidestep the discomfort by clinging to the so-called safety of very certain, low-risk life experiences. Others shrink back, too, but only for a period of time before jumping back into the game. Bouncing back from the inevitable setbacks is the skill of resiliency.

Resilient people respond to setbacks like a beach ball responds to being pushed down into water. If you have ever tried to hold a beach ball down in the water you know that you can try to keep it down, but as soon as there is any opportunity, that ball will find a way to pop back up to the surface. The same is true of resilient people. Like everyone, they will get pushed down from time to time, but as soon as there is an opportunity, they will rebound and pop back up.

We can all relate to the horrible feeling that we get when a plan blows up on us or when our big proposal, the one that we were REALLY counting on to bring in much-needed revenue gets rejected. *UGGGGGH!* Listen, there are times when a period of retreat to regroup—or even mourn—is a healthy and normal response. However, more often than not, what I have seen is that another pattern develops. This pattern creates an internal reinforcement for unhooking from a goal or dream after a setback—in the same way that someone might take a seat on the bench after missing a shot in a big game and then begin to see that seat on the bench as their appropriate, yet far less impactful, place in life.

So here's the deal, folks. As it turns out, life can get pretty messy. In fact, you *want* it to be messy. Even when you deploy the powerful skill of positive expectation that we discussed in the previous chapter, sometimes things still just won't go as you hoped and planned. It happens. That doesn't mean that it is time to abandon your commitment to continuing to expect things to go your way. It just means that, in this particular situation, things didn't go the way you had hoped. Life gets messy. The good news is that frequently, it is from this messiness that your biggest ideas and advancements are born.

The secret is to *embrace* both what we initially see as good, as well as what we initially judge as bad. The secret is to become masterful about resiliency. As you continue to accept the premise that you are inherently connected, protected, guided and loved, then it becomes easier to also accept that every event that shows up in your life holds within it a valuable gift and a powerful lesson custom-made just for you. Your setbacks are an important part of your journey. So, when problems show up, tell yourself that it is OK, all is still well.

When you can see and embrace the gift and lesson in the situations and events that show up in your life, you will now have those as assets and it is that experience that you can use later to propel you past obstacles that would have derailed others. You can learn how to rebound faster, and in this chapter we will identify what it takes to develop and implement that skill in this chapter. For now, if you are processing a setback, hey… power back up, get back in the game, laugh in the face of that so-called setback and start looking for the lessons and gifts. You will find them when you look for them!

"Victory belongs to those who believe in it the most, and believe in it the longest."
—From the movie, Pearl Harbor

Life is about growing, and when things don't go as planned, that's OK—you get do-overs and second chances. This is about catching your second wind when your first wind is knocked out of you. So many people, in the pursuit of their dream, stop short and bail out when they are unknowingly with inches of victory. It is in these times of setback and disappointment that we are vulnerable to Stinkin' Thinkin', those negative thoughts that our ego gladly throws up at us. It is in these times of setback and disappointment that our ego feels most in control and most able to talk us out of holding on and staying the course toward our dream. Remember that disappointment and rejection are part of the experience, especially when you are playing a bigger and bigger game. Resiliency is taking the pain that you experienced and converting that to drive.

Anyone can be a spectator and sit on the sidelines. At least you are in the game—stretching, reaching and striving to be excellent. Hey, you won't always hit the bullseye, you won't always win. Sometimes you are going to fall flat on your face. It's just part of the deal. On the road to greatness, it is not always about winning, though. There will be a measure of failure. Faster success is dependent on a combination of two things: How you accelerate and increase momentum when things are going your way and how well you respond in the times when it feels like the foundation has crumbled beneath your feet.

So, what is your response when there is trouble at the gate? When you hit tough times or unexpected setbacks, do you dig in and summon the Warrior or do you shrink back and surrender? From here on out, no more shrinking back! Summon the unstoppable Warrior that is the essence of who you truly are. It is time to be the Master of Resiliency.

Remember, now and always… *you've got this!*

Failure is not the opposite of success.
It is an important component of success.

There is a need to be resilient in both the micro sense and in the macro sense. "Micro Resiliency" is based on the skills and mindset needed to bounce back from the types of things that can step into our path as we move through the day. "Macro Resiliency" is the set of skills that is needed in order to persevere on a more long-term basis, when bounce-back and recovery from more seemingly significant setbacks are needed.

Micro Resiliency

Sammy is an up and coming junior executive in a London based oil and gas exploration company and a coaching client of Matthews Performance Group. Her daily routine typically includes as many as seven to ten meetings almost back to back. She worked with me to develop new skills that would equip her to be "on", completely present and prepared to deliver as much value as she could in the first meeting of the day, which was sometimes pretty early in the morning and to deliver as much as she could in the very last meeting of the day, which frequently occurred well into the evening. To deliver excellence, a standard to which she was absolutely committed, she figured out a way to be resilient and "on" in each of the segments of each day, regardless of what her schedule was or what events had required her full focus earlier in that same day. Sammy provides an example of the skills and commitment needed to be resilient in the micro sense. This is "Micro Resiliency."

She has a phenomenally busy schedule, just like you probably do, and there are times when she wouldn't mind putting her feet up and kicking back a little bit. But when she has an internal or client meeting coming up, there is no way she is going to show up in some partially-engaged state—no way that she is going to deliver from anything other than her peak operating state. So, in the micro sense, day in and day out, her success relies on her finding out how to create resiliency in any moment.

For Sammy, reaching in and finding the ability to bring her best to each meeting included a three-pronged model in which she:

1. Created a powerful physiology—breathing deeply, holding good posture, smiling more frequently, engaging with appropriate eye contact.
2. Executed from a foundational belief that she was capable and destined to lead, inspire, challenge, connect and succeed. She

placed her focus on past experiences when she had "nailed it," avoiding the trap so many fall into of focusing on the times in the past when they failed, dropped the ball or simply didn't stay strong.

3. Memorized her own Power Up Sequence, a small, unique and personalized set of phrases she developed that anchored her deeply to her core, her values, and her sense of being connected, protected, guided and loved.

Macro Resiliency

It is also important to be able to create resiliency in the bigger span of your life—in the macro sense, "Macro resiliency". As we are going to discuss later in this chapter, there are times when we are going to hit setbacks, we're going to hit low energy, we're going to experience disappointments. We're going to go through times when it won't be easy to recoil, to rebound, to move forward with passion. These are the times when you will want to have some new tools to help you create resiliency in this bigger aspect of your life, especially when the stakes are high.

Remember this....

"In life, it's not how hard you can hit,
it's how hard a hit you can take."
—From the movie *Creed*

The way you show up in the little things is how you will show up in the bigger things. In other words, the way you show up creating resiliency in the different parts of your day (Micro) is how you'll show up creating resiliency when you need it most—when a big (Macro), unexpected setback occurs, when there is a serious disturbance in the "Force".

Why Is Resiliency Important?

Resiliency is the accelerator for happiness. Through my mentors, I have been given a powerful gift, one for which I am deeply grateful. In the very moment that I am learning about a problem or setback, I am already wondering how I am going to reframe the situation so that I can move forward to create a great situation despite the current setback. This skill is what has shifted my response to challenges. It's an important skill for success, and I will teach you how to employ it too.

When you understand the resiliency and acceleration formula and become adept in your ability to quickly catch your second wind, you'll not only get more of the results that you want, but you'll also be more deeply anchored to your power through the clarity of knowing that your achievement and fulfillment all start and end with your choices, thoughts, and decisions.

The good news is that resiliency is a natural phenomenon. Let's look at some examples. Immediately following a forest fire, the land initiates the process of growing new trees to replace those lost in the fire. The increase in available sunlight that results from the old trees being destroyed accelerates the germination of seeds that were covered up, waiting quietly in the ground for their chance to grow. Clear out the old, start the new—that's the process for rebuilding the forest as quickly as possible. The ecosystem is amazingly resilient, and it doesn't wait to start rebuilding.

Like the forest, you are already healing from whatever has injured you, even though you might not be aware of it. Healing and recovery are as natural as breathing. Think about it. When you cut your finger, in the first seconds immediately following the occurrence of that cut, your body initiates the healing process without your having to consciously do anything. First, your body works to limit blood loss by reducing the amount of blood flowing to the wounded area. Next, proteins in your blood work with your platelets and plasma to form a protective covering called a scab (*yuck, but awesome!*) which acts to protect the wound from outside infection. White blood cells are dispatched to the area to further battle infection. Your skin begins to regenerate and, voilà... the wound is healed. Your body is resilient—it doesn't wait to start rebuilding.

You also possess the ability to begin healing from every emotional and mental wound—and to recover from any disappointment or setback within seconds. When people have the mental and emotional strength needed to move past disasters such as the devastation and loss from earthquakes or other such natural occurrences, the pain of failed relationships, the discouragement of a lost business or opportunity, or the challenges of a health problem, their lives become more full of joy, happiness and success. They find within them a power and strength that without experiencing the challenge, they wouldn't have known that they had.

The ability to rebound is an outward expression of confidence and trust that the strength exists within us to pick up the pieces and move forward, even when we aren't exactly sure where we are going to find that strength. What differentiates those that persevere through tough situations and setbacks from those that throw in the towel, give up on their dreams and give up on themselves? It is simply one thing—they have figured out how to be resilient—they don't wait to start rebuilding.

Given This, Now What Will I Do?

Last year I was in a large meeting room with seven or eight hundred people. In the crowd I could see many faces, but one really stood out. It was the face of a young woman who appeared to be in her early twenties. Energy, warmth, love and confidence seemed to radiate from her. She was sitting up in her seat, taking everything in with an enthusiasm that

I have seldom seen. I could see that others had also noticed her presence and energy. I thought, "Wow, she must really have life by the tail. She is young, beautiful, engaging, fit, with a good sense of style—and she's obviously considerate and a great example to those whom she meets."

As the meeting wrapped up, I was talking to another person who had attended the seminar and as we finished our discussion, out of the corner of my eye, I caught a glimpse of her and her friends as they were getting ready to leave the room. I noticed that she was the last one to get up out of her chair, and it became clear why as she stood up, grabbed her crutches and entered the aisle. She was missing one leg. I learned later that her leg had been amputated following a car accident in which the car she was in was hit by a drunk driver.

I could hardly reconcile what she had gone through with the one-in-a-million attitude and radiance that she so clearly possessed. She was a living example of one of the primary components of living a life of resiliency. That component is simple—it is the skill of asking ourselves better questions.

She could have easily, and understandably, brought her focus to a question like, "Why did this happen to me?" or "Why was I the one that lost a leg?" We would all certainly empathize with her, and we would also easily feel sorry for her. But she chose a different, more powerful question. This kind of physical condition could not be reversed or cured. Her leg was gone forever. She, like many others with similar physical setbacks, had an important question to ask and answer, and it is the same one that we must all answer in the face of a setback, "Given this, now what do I do?"

It would be easy for any of us to understand if this young woman had turned bitter and withdrawn following the amputation of her leg, knowing how much that would change her future. But she had obviously decided to take a different path. Sometimes things happen that we would give anything to reverse. But we can't. And we are faced with a decision—stay in the game or sit it out. She was a phenomenally resilient person who obviously didn't wait to start rebuilding.

So, just like this young woman—you have a choice. You can choose to focus on what you don't have—or focus on what you do have. If you are habitually deeply celebrating what you have, happiness will be yours even when you are navigating through difficult times. If you choose to focus instead on what you *don't* have, what's *not* working out for you or how whatever happened to you was not fair, you will never find peace—and you will certainly miss the best that life has in store for you.

The great news is that whether you are naturally prone to bouncing back quickly or not, resiliency is a skill that can be learned and improved upon. And when you display resiliency, you are training the universe that you are ready to kick back into gear as fast as possible. You are telling the universe that you have no need for prolonged recuperation or to sit out the rest of the game. In response, the universe will send new and better opportunities for you to experience immediately. Why? That's right... because the universe will know that you are resilient and that you won't wait to start rebuilding.

We are not defined by what happens to us in life. What defines us is how graciously and powerfully we move on and stay in the game. There is always an open spot waiting for you on the sidelines. The other spectators will welcome you in. When things get difficult, the question becomes, "Are you one that will shake off the dirt and move on, or are you someone who will bail and take a seat in the bleachers?"

Among the most powerful questions:
"Given this, now what will you do?"

How to Build Your Resiliency Muscles

You can start taking control and reducing the length of time that you are knocked off balance (and perhaps knocked out of the game) in any of the following points in the cycle of moving through disappointment, setbacks and tough times:

1. Before a setback or disappointment occurs
2. At the time a setback or disappointment shows up
3. In the time that follows a setback or disappointment

The Warrior skills, beliefs and attitudes will help lift us out of the grasp of disappointing and difficult times. These are the same skills that we tap into when things are going well and we want to keep our momentum building. They appear to be different only because of the mental environment that we are experiencing during these two dramatically different points in the success cycle. Remember, setbacks and disappointments are just part of the success cycle.

In one case we are re-establishing momentum, while in the other, we are accelerating momentum. In the previous chapter, we identified empowering and disempowering patterns. Let's have a look at some additional patterns to be on the lookout for that will support or delay the likelihood that you will rebound quickly. Let's move your focus to the ways that you have chosen to condition yourself to react to the events and experiences in your life so that you can become more aware of any existing positive and negative patterns. We will explore processes that will help you capitalize on your strength-building rituals and eliminate the ones that are holding you back.

Before a Setback Occurs

Preparing yourself for the tough stuff before it shows up in your life is critical. Preparing mentally and emotionally for *some* level of setback and failure helps keep you from getting knocked as far off balance, and it shortens recovery time. In conditioning yourself by thinking through exactly how you will respond to the Crap Storm *before* it hits, you will be ready when it happens with a well-thought-through and specific sequence of conditioned responses. I know, I know... this seems like it is in conflict with the "Law of Attraction" and other similar philosophies which advise that what we put our focus on is what we get.

I can understand that there could be some confusion. But here's the deal: Most of us will put some focus on thoughts of failure, whether we are conscious of that or not. By carving out a relatively small amount of time to bring the possibility of failure to the forefront of our minds so that we can proactively build our recovery plan, we are shortening the amount of time and energy that will be required in the event of failure. Think it through in advance, build the plan for rebounding, move on!

Step 1: Prepare your *Bounce Back Strategy*. Imagine holding two balls, one in each hand. One made of glass and the other made of rubber. Imagine letting go of both balls and watching them fall to the floor. When the glass ball contacts the hard surface, it shatters, while the rubber ball takes the shock and bounces back up and into your hand. Resiliency. It shows what you are made of—fragile glass or flexible rubber. What strengths and natural attributes do you possess that help you bounce back? Acknowledge and list those strengths and count them as part of your Bounce Back Strategy.

Step 2: Prepare your attitude. A sales leader that I worked closely with had a motto that helped him bounce back instantly from the many opportunities for rejection that go along with the sales profession. Whether he was having a great day advancing and closing deals or a bad day when no one was saying "Yes" to him, he would say this over and over:

"Some will, some won't. Who cares, who's next?"

I heard him say that so many times that it stayed in my consciousness even when I was away from the office, but it is powerful. By the way, when he said, "Who cares," he never meant that he didn't care about the customers, their best interests or the sales process. He meant, "Whatever the response, it will not affect my state of mind or my momentum."

Step 3: Prepare your resiliency environment—including music, videos, quotes, photos. Remember this important point from the previous chapter? Self-empowerment is not an exclusively cerebral game. There are things you can do in your physical environment to empower yourself. Consider these when you want to recover quickly: What helps you think big? What are your favorite songs that get you pumped up and energized? This is your Power Up music! What kind of visuals help you feel empowered? Does exercise make you feel stronger, more positive and energetic? How about conversation? What friendships or mentors are your huge fans—the ones that make you feel great and build you up when you see and talk with them?

It's up to you to consciously, deliberately—with every move you make, set yourself up to win. So, pay attention to the environment you're creating in every moment, in every situation, and deliberately be the creator of that environment. Be sure what you create jazzes you, inspires you, brings you back to thinking big!

"You can't control the wind, but you can adjust your sails."
—Yiddish Proverb

Step 4: Know who your "Make It Happen People" are and reciprocate. Identify and routinely connect with at least one person that can always pull you out of a slump. Create a "standby agreement" with that person and, of course, make a point of also being available to support them personally.

Remember, the best time to prepare to catch your second wind is before your first wind fades. Until you build a different response, you won't have a different experience when tough times hit. When you get an unexpected punch to the gut, how long will you stay doubled over before you stand back up and start walking it off?

It is really important to have yourself prepared for the inevitable tough times that are most certainly part of any sustained endeavor. Resiliency is the outward expression of your internal fortitude and strength.

At the Time of a Setback

Is there a time to quit, to throw in the towel? Maybe. Is this the time for that? Hell no! The only way to find out for sure is to immediately get back in the fight. When a setback occurs, it is more important than ever to access and activate your Warrior attitude: "I am much stronger than this problem, way more powerful than this setback. I am a Warrior!"

Famous Cookies

Wally Amos, famous for his very successful cookie business, put it this way, "One thought that is always uppermost in my mind is this: If I stop, I am sure to lose everything I have invested in my idea. I don't know what may happen or whom I may meet if I just keep going one more second, one more day, or one more week. It is impossible to know who is heading my way with a piece of my answer. I constantly remind myself that there are no facts concerning the future. It is always in the process of development."

Being able to catch your second wind when roadblocks appear and setbacks or disappointments show up provides you with a powerful advantage because when you can reduce the amount of time that you are sidetracked, waiting to recover and rebound, you have increased your productive time and decreased the wear and tear on your most essential, critical attributes—your emotional strength, your attitude and your sense of being unstoppable. Notice what follows in the moments that follow setbacks.

Step 1: Regain Clear Vision

Get above the storm to get a glimpse of the horizon in the distance. The minutiae of this moment is merely so much dust swirling around you, obstructing your vision and taking your focus off what is most important. It will pass and you will be stronger for having ridden through it. Start by connecting to your big "What's." What did you come here to contribute? What are you committed to achieving in this pass through life? What is the higher purpose and how might this setback actually support your ultimate achievement of that higher purpose?

This first step in the moments that a setback is in motion requires regaining clarity of your vision and purpose. It's time to get a better look at what is happening, a reality check. To be able to really see what is going on, you'll need both a microscope and a telescope. Clarity within the minutia, as well as clarity of the big picture, are equally important. Sometimes it is better to focus on what is right in front of you and what demands your immediate attention, while other times it is more important to look at the horizon and reconnect to your big mission. The key is to know when to focus on what is close and when to focus on what is farther away, off in the distance—the bigger picture. So, clean your lenses, get your clear vision back.

By the way, remember that others look to you for insight about how to deal with challenges and tough times. In life, and in every day, you are either an example—or a warning. While we certainly notice how those that we admire thrive during times when things are going well, we often get the deepest insight into someone's character by observing how they respond when the s*#t hits the fan. We seek to see and experience the strength that others are able to conjure up when they are faced with difficult and troubling times. What are they accessing that helps them get through it and thrive once again? Your struggles and hard times, after all, test your ability and your resolve.

If you think about it, our favorite movies are often based on a theme of resilience and the ability to bounce back. Everyone cheered in *Top Gun* when Maverick, played by Tom Cruise, re-engaged in the final air battle. "Talk to me, Goose; talk to me, Goose... Maverick is re-engaging, Sir!" This was the huge recovery scene in the movie. We all know that problems are going to pop up. That is a given. What inspires us most is how our heroes come back from those challenges. It is not the *problems* that someone faces that we remember nearly as much as it is their resiliency in the face of them.

Who are the people that are looking to you, observing your response to setbacks—family, friends, coworkers, your team, those in leadership positions above you?

Step 2: Get focused on solutions

You know that at some point in the future you will figure out a solution to whatever challenge you are facing. Now is the time to learn the shortcuts so that you can speed up that process. Ask yourself these questions, "If there were a solution to this, what would it be?" and "What can I choose to do, think and believe about myself and my place in this world in order to get back to attracting the outcomes that I want?"

Right now you have the power to shift from "insecure" to "in control," from "self-questioning" to "self confident," from wanting to quit to locking in an even bigger vision for your life. What's it going to be? Are you powerful or powerless? You now know that once a "rule" or a belief is internalized, your mind will seek out and find evidence to validate that belief. It may be that you have convinced yourself that you have a limit that in reality you don't.

This is why getting focused is imperative whenever you encounter a setback. Take a hard look at your already-internalized beliefs and decide which new ones will serve you better now.

Setbacks and disappointments can trigger worry, a sense that this setback now makes us vulnerable and that our future is now more bleak. We worry that in some future time we will be helpless, with more and more things being out of our control. Now is the time to create strong focus. Your primary responsibility in this phase is to maintain the light burning inside of you. No one else can keep you in the game except you. In times of uncertainty and doubt it is more important than ever to keep your focus on the present, what you can and will do now. In this moment you are OK. You are not starving, you are not on the street— you are OK in *THIS* moment, and right now the choice to be resilient is all yours!

Step 3: Activate your Bounce Strategy

In the prior section where we outlined what to do "Before a Setback Occurs", you prepared your Bounce Back Strategy. Now is the time to move into action. Activate your Bounce Back Strategy. This is the time to be completely honest with yourself and ask, "What will move me forward in this moment? What is the right action, right now? What will it take for me to bounce back?"

Focus on what you need next. Action brings power. Recognize the gaps in your knowledge, resources and contacts that led to the setback... and get busy filling in those gaps. Declare out loud what you want to attract, expect it to show up, trust and believe that it will. Then notice what shows up—and capitalize on it.

There is absolutely NO reason to let thoughts of hurdles and disappointment stay in your consciousness for more than a few seconds. Some folks have a habit of ruminating on the hurdles in front of them or the disappointments of the past. This is not you. You have a *Bounce Back* mentality now. This is when it's critical to remember... *You've Got This!*

POWER-UP QUESTION

Getting back up, dusting yourself off and getting back in the fight is simply a choice. There are tough days and there are turnaround days. Which one are you going to make this day?

Quick, answer the next three questions pronto!

- What is the story that you are telling yourself about this bummer of a situation?
- What are you making WAY bigger than it is?
- What do you still need to clean up?

Step 4: No coincidences

Everything that we experience as we travel through this crazy life, this journey, shows up for a reason. My personal belief is that there are no coincidences. It is crystal clear to me that nothing happens without a reason, and there are multiple opportunities in every situation IF that is what you are looking for and expecting.

A presupposition that things show up in our lives to help us expand and build strength will serve us both now and in the future. Embracing this mindset creates positive hormonal responses as we process the event through the lens of optimism and hope. The hormones that are released as a result actually open up creative parts of your brain, which in turn, help you identify solutions that are simply missed by those who embrace a negative, victim mindset.

Let's take a close look at that victim mindset. A presupposition that we are powerless and that things happen *to* us, not *for* us, shuts down important mental and emotional processing and reduces our resiliency. This brings to the fore an important question: Is it possible that one's mindset creates and even determines one's expectations— and that one's expectations then create and determine one's actions, results and fulfillment?

I believe that mindset determines fulfillment and results— because I have seen the results of each type of mindset play out over and over again. There is a big difference between, "Why me?" and "What is the gift and lesson in this for me?" I firmly believe that the gift is always greater than the pain or the inconvenience of your setback.

The anticipation of a problem being insurmountable begets an insurmountable problem. Naturally. So, keep strong guards at the castle walls and a vigilant lookout for opportunities, even in the midst of things that show up that you don't like. They are often blessings in disguise.

After a Setback Occurs

Whoa—what was THAT all about? Lost your job, lost an important customer, your marriage cratered, unexpected health problem? Forensic work is called for after a setback. Be curious versus judgmental in your assessment—and be thorough. Real rigor is necessary now. Here are the steps to take to understand the "what" and "why" of what just happened so that you can regain your footing, and if possible, avoid repeating those mistakes that you may have contributed that brought on the setback. Sometimes, of course, setbacks happen even though you had no conscious role in them. It happens. But it still pays to be open to carefully examining all possible causative factors.

Here are the steps of your forensic analysis. Just like any other forensic procedure, it starts with a step-by-step examination.

Step 1: When things got tough, what did I allow to take me out of the zone?

Step 2: What did I learn that I can use to rebound faster next time I encounter a setback?

Step 3: What is the meaning that I have assigned to the events that occurred?

Step 4: Were there specific mental or emotional shifts that I made as I reacted to those events?

Step 5: Summon the Warrior and initiate massive action—even when you feel a tug to pull back and unhook. What are one BIG THING and one LITTLE THING that you can do right now to re-establish momentum?

Ask yourself what you would have to believe in order to jump back into the game with a big smile on your face right now. Need some data? OK, here's a fact for you: So many people stop just short (millimeters!) of getting what they want. I've seen this happen so many times. If they had just stayed on the path for a few extra steps, they would have crossed over to what they wanted. Sometimes it takes a ton of faith to get back in the game and see the possibilities. Even though some folks don't know it in the moment, many of them quit when they are almost at the finish line because of an untimely setback. Remember what Wally Amos told us—one more big push, one more month of staying on course is what makes all the difference. So, step back up and Power Up!

What Can Derail You and Squash Resilience?
Settling

Many dabble in the apparent pursuit of a dream only to retreat to the safety zone after the first or second (or third) setback. What is that about? When insecurity is running the show, we begin to shut life down. We are not as likely to step up, step out, stretch and explore. Focus shifts from possibility and growth to seeking security and certainty. This is when the doors to settling fly open and try to lure us in. Settling makes us feel safe—but in the big picture, the price you pay is HUGE!

How many times in your life have you assigned disproportionate meaning to something, and then let the meaning that you assigned keep you from reaching out and creating what you wanted?

> It's not until you are right at the point where you are about to give it all up that you come face to face with your highest level of courage.

For some, reaching and going for what they want is scary. It becomes scarier when we get closer to actually creating the new life, the new level of fitness, the new business, relationship or career that we want. When we catch a glimpse, there is often a part of us that freaks out because instead of just talking about making something new and cool for ourselves, *whoa*, we are actually faced with doing it and with the possibility of succeeding or failing. That means that we are forever raising the bar, leaving the comfort of mediocrity behind—and yeah, that's scary. The reflexive answer? Pull back to the "known normal" ASAP. But that just isn't you any more, right?

Dark Moments, Dark Times

Have you ever been in a situation where things seemed so bleak that you thought, "I don't know what to do anymore, I really don't."

It's important to become aware of what you say to yourself—especially when you have had a failure, but also when you succeed. When you are in the wake of a recent failure, be on the lookout for the negative things that you've become habitually accustomed to saying to yourself—and then asking yourself, "Where is that coming from? My spirit or my pesky, insecure ego?" You'll know!

Here's a good practice: The next time you experience a setback or a success, notice what you say to yourself. Write it down. When it's a negative dialogue, when your ego's taken over and is whispering nonsense to you again, stop a moment and check it out. Is this real? Is it relative—or important? The setback is over, so shorten your down time and deliver your attention to your internal "success dialogue" instead. This is what you need to emphasize. Certainly, you'll get knocked down from time to time, you're human, but getting back up fast is possibly the most important of all success skills.

You know, you can change those old tapes out—just like you would in any type of playback machine. Have you ever lulled yourself into making your problems worse by saying, "Man, this is terrible" or "I have really screwed up now" or "See, I knew this would happen." Time to upgrade the tape. "What is the best and fastest way to rectify this situation?" and "No worries, *I've got this*—I'm back, starting right now." Your words matter! Change your tape.

When you are thinking, "Oh, the hell with this—this is just too much. I quit, I'm done, over and out." Really? Let's get just a little perspective please! How does *your* problem stack up with the no-clean-water, no-food-to-eat today crowd?

Setbacks provide us with an excuse
to quit or a chance to double down.

Sometimes the real challenge is that quitting can feel really comfortable. Retreating in a big way can be inviting because we get to relax, wallow, and basically unhook, not have to perform, not have to deliver. It's like finally setting down two huge, heavy suitcases with sharp, painful handles. And guess what else... some of your friends and family members will support you on your return to the status quo because, frankly, your going for it, stretching yourself and expanding may have made them uncomfortable deep down.

Remember, there is always room for you on the bench or in the stands. The problem is that tucked inside those very same suitcases that you will be dropping, layered in among all the stuff that you have come to resent, are the very dreams that called to you when you decided to go for your dream. If you walk away from those suitcases, you will also walk away from the part of you that knows there is more for you.

Resiliency is a choice. Your choice. Yesterday is over. Your "failures" are forgiven. The lessons learned are in place. The score is Zero/Zero. To get back into the game, start doing the most important things right now. You have to participate in your own rescue. No Pity Party—it's over!

YOU CAN START TODAY

With your forensic analysis complete and your lessons identified, direct your full attention to what is in front of you. Deploy your biggest assets, the ones that NOBODY can ever take from you—your energy and skill—to your biggest advantage. Future focus! You have identified the lessons, figured out what knocked you out of the zone and there is no more value to be had in fixating on the past. You can't afford to have 30%, 40% or 50% of your energy and focus looking back toward the past. Turn 100% of your energy to moving forward. No excuses. No regrets. No judgment. Nothing more will be served by your staying in the weeds and focusing on how things "should have gone" for even one more second.

Now, is the time to focus on what you can and will you do in the next hour, day, week and year!

Resiliency Tool # 1: Your Success Formula

Decide what the basics are for you in this situation. It's time to build out your Success Formula. Whether you loved math and science back in school or hated it, you probably at least admired the value of knowing that there was a specific answer to *any* problem that your teacher presented to you. As long as you identified the right formula, you could solve the problem and get to the right answer. The same is true when you find yourself feeling stuck or frustrated or just bummed out. There is always at least one solution to any problem that you encounter. Shift your attention to finding the solution, and you will move out of the fog and get solidly back in the game.

Getting unstuck happens faster when we get super clear about the small handful of actions that we can and will take. This is called "chunking down" the problem into solvable terms. So, here is what this Success Formula looks like:

$$\underline{\hspace{2cm}} + \underline{\hspace{1.5cm}} + \underline{\hspace{1.5cm}} = \underline{\hspace{3cm}}$$

(Action/Shift) + (Action/Shift) + (Action/Shift) = (Desired outcome or result)

Now, let's lay out your Success Formula. On a clean sheet of paper write the following:

1. Put an equal sign (=) in the middle of the top line of the page.
2. Next, write out the outcome(s) that you want. For instance your "=" could be something like "= Bring in our next $25,000 client, or fall in love, or start a new career, or build your health and fitness back following a medical challenge."
3. On the left side of the equal sign complete the equation with two (or more) things that need to be in place/developed/maximized/enhanced in order to get the outcome listed on the right side of the equal sign. It is that simple.

Example:

Contacting 50 brand new prospective clients/week
+ Creating massive, focus and optimism on the team
+ Tightening up and delivering an over-the-top, powerful, compelling value proposition
= Bringing in our next $ 25,000 client"

Okay, you've defined your near-term Success Formula. *You've got this!* Now it is time to implement.

Resiliency Tool # 2: "While" Is a Powerful Word

Sometimes you will find that there is more than one solution that will get you to your desired future experience. And other times there may be what seem to be conflicting or competing paths that lie in front of you. To increase our ability to be resilient, we need to become more and more nimble. Seeing various possible solutions to a problem that we are facing helps us be more positive and more nimble. When we feel that we are in a corner or must make a decision between one desired outcome or another, our field of vision can become narrow to the point where we only see two choices available to us—choose this path or take that path, pursue this opportunity *or* pursue that other opportunity. This limited thinking leads to seeing only "this or that" and can conceal a third option which is "this *and* that".

Let me show you what I mean.

Third Option Example # 1: "Should I start up my new business now or stay with my corporate job?" becomes "How can I launch my new business and satisfy my desire to be an entrepreneur *while* still maintaining the income and benefits that I like?" Rather than only an "either/or" decision, you can create additional options. In this case, new options might include working on your business launch at night and on weekends while continuing to be a top performer in your "day job" or being the new business owner but not the new business operator, leveraging, instead, someone else's time, energy and expertise to run the business.

Third Option Example # 2: "Should I go to the game with my friends or spend time with my sister?" becomes "How can I go to the game with my friends *while* also connecting with my sister?" New options appear, including perhaps, having your sister join you for the game with your friends. What decision are you working through right now? How can you discover new options by restating your questions using the "*while*" model? Try it—you'll be surprised how it opens up your options.

Resiliency Tool # 3: Be Open to Miracles
The Miracle of a Nickel

When my professional development company was about two years old, we hit a short period of time where money got tight. I had a son in his twenties, a son in college, and two more children at home. My wife was home with our two younger ones, so our income and lifestyle were completely generated from the business. While it is true that my business was growing, we still found ourselves in a very uncomfortable situation financially.

At the time, I officed from home. My office window faced the street, and one day as I was finishing up a proposal that I wanted to get out right away, I saw our mail carrier arrive. "Oh well," I thought to myself, "there's a drop-off box a block away and pickup's at 5:00 p.m." So, I completed the final touches and headed out to drop off my package. As I turned around to go back home, I noticed a nickel lying on the street. In that moment, I remembered my dad and his philosophy about whether or not to pick up coins on the street.

If we were together and saw a coin on the ground, and if I or one of my brothers hadn't reached down to pick up the coin, Dad would pick it up, and then he'd say, "I'll tell you what, I will pick up all of the coins that we come across and you pick up all of the bills—and in the end, guess who will come out richer? Me!" That made a lot of sense to me, so from childhood to this day, I always pick up coins when I see them.

Naturally, I picked up the nickel and, as I was walking home, I rubbed it between my fingers as though it had some kind of mystical power, like a touchstone or Aladdin's lamp. I returned to my office and, almost without being fully conscious about what I was doing or why, I taped that nickel up on a big whiteboard that I had on the wall. I then picked up a marker and right next to the nickel wrote, "Here comes my next $5,000."

I didn't think much about it after that as I prepared for my next coaching call. About halfway through that call, again, not fully aware of what I was doing, I grabbed the eraser and changed the "$5,000" to "$100,000." The sentence now read, "Here comes my next $100,000."

As my conversation on the phone ended I sat back in my chair and looked back up at that nickel and thought, "Wow, $100,000! That is way more exciting." I went on to the next call, and the one after that, and then left the office for the night.

Back in my office the next day, the coin would occasionally catch my eye and I would read the sentence again, "Here comes my next

$100,000." I must have read that twenty or more times that day—and the following day, as well—really not thinking much about it except that that $100,000 would sure be awesome to have, given our financial situation.

Toward the end of the second day after I'd taped the newly found nickel on the whiteboard and written (then rewritten) the sentence next to it, I received a call from a person I had been talking to about a project. He informed me that I had been selected for the engagement—and the contract value for the first twelve months was $103,000!

> For there to be magic in your world,
> you must first believe in magic.

Call it magic, call it luck, call it blessings, call it hard work paying off... what is important is that you are open more and more to having support coming to you from the outside in.

Resiliency Tool # 4: Build Unstoppable Momentum
(Source: *Expanding the Glimpse* Audio Program produced by Matthews Performance Group)

Have you ever noticed that it's easy to spot a person who's on track, all in and advancing toward his or her mission? You can tell just by looking at them that they are dialed in, tuned in, powered up and unstoppable. And most often these people, the ones tuned in to their mission, are peak performers getting—and also giving—at high levels.

What is it that you notice about a person who is on their mission and in sync with their vision? What sets them apart? What sets *you* apart from the pack when you are connected to and delivering on your mission and vision? That's right, it's the way you show up. To begin with, it's the way that you show up physically. Even your walk is deliberate and purposeful, you are keenly aware of where you are going and all that is happening around you.

Mentally, the unstoppable person is not scattered and disengaged—they are alert and completely in the present moment. Even though they may have been up late the night before putting the final touches on a big proposal or finishing a project, they appear sharp and rested. They don't miss details and, when an obstacle comes up—something that would have led some to give up—they are on it and effortlessly resourceful, providing new solutions, almost on the fly. What would have been a mountain to someone else becomes no more than a bump in the road for them. They lead themselves or their teams with compassion, while at the same time, holding an expectation that people will pull through for them. It is almost like a sixth sense; they are accessing their mental genius and making excellent decisions. Things seem to end up going their way. Just like a puzzle, each piece eventually falls into place.

You've had that feeling before and you know what I'm talking about. What could you accomplish in your life if you were in that powerful, focused, deliberate state more often—a powerful frame of mind, a mindset that you counted on to determine what you did, how you spent your time, whose words and perspectives you allowed in and which ones you filtered out?

That is what the "Building Unstoppable Momentum" tool has been designed to do—to put you in that state, in that place whenever and wherever you want it. And yes, that is absolutely accessible to you every second of every day.

To get maximum results from this day, start by recognizing what your strengths and weaknesses are in that moment. Knowing your points of power, as well as the gaps that exist between how you are showing up in that moment and how you would prefer to show up, is valuable because when you know where the gaps are, then you can make the adjustments necessary to assure top performance and, more importantly, attract, create and develop exactly what you most want.

Right now, imagine yourself as an Olympic 400-meter runner at the starting line of a big race. Imagine that you woke up feeling completely rested and ready for the race, your shoes feel tight and comfortable, the weather is perfect and you feel strong. You know that you have the edge, you are ready to win! Now all that remains is the execution.

What would it be like if you were to feel that you possess everything that it takes to win right now?

You can build and keep unstoppable momentum by launching every day with a check-in with what is already aligned for success and what needs to be adjusted. Just like a chiropractor adjusts your spine for health, you have the ability and the responsibility to adjust your attitude, strength, expectations and your physical, emotional, intellectual, and even spiritual body.

Here is how this works. Take a few minutes right now to rate yourself in each of the following areas. Be completely honest and objective. This is not about recognizing how you SHOULD feel, but how you actually DO feel!

Rate yourself using a scale of 1 to 10 with 1 being "I am completely out of the game" and 10 being "I am ready to crush it today!"

_____ I know exactly what I will do today to get exceptional results.

_____ My attitude is dialed in and adjusted for success.

_____ I feel physically strong and full of energy.

_____ I worked out this morning (OK, or last night).

_____ I slept well and for the right amount of time, I'm eating healthy and drinking water to remain fully hydrated.

_____ My emotional state is aligned and supporting my mission. My primary emotion right now is_____.

_____ I am mentally sharp, intense, determined and FOCUSED.

_____ What is on my "To-Do" list is relevant and will move me toward my long-term goals.

_____ My schedule is aggressive and deliberate.

_____ I feel connected, protected, guided and loved. YES!!

_____ I am committed to doing whatever it takes to succeed—upholding high morals, ethics and standards.

_____ I have a positive expectation that clients, customers, team members, and others will pull through for me, as I will also pull through for them.

_____ I am a Warrior and I will make today outstanding!

_____ TOTAL SCORE

110 – 130: You are Unstoppable! Get out there and create huge impact. Average: 8 – 10

90 – 109: Not bad, not bad at all. You're positioned to have a productive day. Average: 7 – 8

70 – 89: Above the mean. What can you do to step it up a bit more? Average: 6 - 7

50 – 69: Your habits and lifestyle may be holding you back. What needs to be addressed? Average: 4 – 5

Under 50: Yikes! In the danger zone here. What can you do to advance your score in at least one of the thirteen categories listed? Make it a MUST. As you do, your momentum will increase. Average: 0 – 4

So, how did you score on this exercise? Each of these questions is designed to help you get clear about what is already in alignment and geared for great results and to let you know what areas need attention and adjustment. You see, you can have a great attitude, but if you take half of the morning bouncing around because you don't know what to do next, you're ineffective. Or if you know exactly what to do but are fatigued, stressed and in low energy, you're not set up for success either.

I believe that your power to attract what you want in your life, to open yourself to receive even more is dramatically enhanced when you couple your clarity and expectation and the power of attraction with large-scale action. Clarity and action combined help you develop unstoppable momentum. What would it take to get more of the Unstoppable Momentum categories up into the 8 zone, up into the 9 zone, up into the 10 zone? When you do, you amplify your power and your results. You become the powerful, unstoppable person you've seen in others many times. This time it will be you.

Now, continue to do this exercise at the start of your day—either before or as soon as you arrive at your workspace; in other words, wherever it is that you shift into productive mode. It is important to do this before other activities and distractions break into your world. As you embrace this exercise you will notice that it will energize you, focus you, and set the stage for a phenomenal day. Do this every day and you will notice the difference in your progress—and your success.

Attitude absolutely effects resiliency. Mastering resiliency absolutely determines results.

Mastering Resiliency is a choice.
Don't give up, don't give in.
Reach down deep and catch your second wind!

There are times when getting back in the game is the right move. Sometimes though, it turns out that you are in the wrong game. Let's take a look at ways you can tell the difference and manage through transitions when this is the case.

Chapter 5

Reinvent Yourself
Initiating Big Change

*"So often times it happens that we live our lives in chains
And we never even know we have the key..."*
—The Eagles

What is reinventing?

Reinvention is simply deliberate evolution. It is the determination to embrace a new life direction. It will require you to expand, and the payoff is that as you do, so does the potential for new and exciting opportunities to come forward. It takes a leap of faith to initiate change and to pursue something new without the benefit of knowing for sure if the new path will pan out for you.

In this section, we're going to explore how to successfully make that kind of shift and how doing it can lead to breaking through the barriers that have stood between you and your desires.

Reinvention is also a deliberate rejection of the status quo. Sometimes as life unfolds, course corrections are needed. You've got to change some stuff up—and not just for the variety of it, but because the path that you are on is simply not getting you where you want to go. When that is the case, you are at one of your most important crossroads and you have a decision to make. You can continue to walk down the existing path, or you can recognize the calling and shift your course. When you know in your heart that change is needed in order for you to live your life at a more meaningful level, build out your new plan and get busy transitioning. Bouncing along and living an "OK, not-bad life" is NOT how you want to spend your life, is it? If any part of your life is not what you want it to be, then the...*status quo has got to go!*

My deepest wish for you—and the driving force behind the creation of this book—is that you become more and more aware of opportunities to be brave as they show up in your life. I hope you'll embrace those moments as the gifts that they are and learn to make the internal shifts necessary to experience life at a new, outrageously phenomenal level. Reinvention is another call to be brave.

Reinventing oneself is always an available option. The idea of reinventing yourself can be scary as hell, though, and for some people, it's the reason they won't do it—but for others, that is why they *must* do it. It is not for everyone, especially those who place high value on certainty, consistency and comfort. If certainty, consistency and comfort are very, very important to you, then that's 100% OK. Skip this chapter and flip to Chapter 6.

Still here? Outstanding! Being able to take on some uncertainty is critical to success. Uncertainty can be uncomfortable, and in the words of my son Bradon, "Comfort and happiness are not the same thing." That is so true. While it is quite comfortable to travel a path that we have traveled before, one that we know so well, it is not in the comfort of repeating past experiences but rather in those times when we are striving and reaching and learning new things that we are often most inspired.

What differentiates those who are living life with passion, success, and joy from those who are simply settling? The answer is that those living full out have figured out how to attach deeply to their dreams—*and here's the key*—they have been brave enough to hold themselves to a high standard and to reinvent themselves when it became necessary. This has created a magnetic pull, attracting success and joy to fill their lives. They have a different belief about what is possible. You can only know what is possible for you by walking across the line that separates the known from the unknown. Scary? Oftentimes, yes.

What do you need to know about successfully changing course?

Left to common thinking, we can find ourselves subscribing to the belief that the path that we are on is the path that we must remain on forever. There are many stories that people will tell themselves in order to feel better about eliminating options for growth and change. We self-impose limiting rules like, "I am too old now" or "I am too young to pull this off" or "I have never done something like this before—I can't do this." I am a huge fan of reality testing, which is taking the time to check in with yourself, your coach, your advisory team, to validate that your plans and timelines are realistic. What is not OK with me, and should not be OK with you, is playing small under the guise of being "a realist" or because of the "rules" that we carry around with us. Here's the key thing to remember about your rules:

**R.U.L.E.S. are Reasons Usually Linked
to Embracing the Status Quo**

What opportunities do you wish you had pursued, but didn't? Are there openings that have shown up in the past, offering a chance to step into a more exciting version of your life—but you let them slide? What possibilities did you reject and eliminate from the pool of possible experiences because of your own internal rules?

There are few things more unsettling for me than to know that so many among us walk the path that we are on, not because it is our bliss, but instead, because we are terrified of change or concerned about what others would think of us.

The details of your current situation, just like everything in your life, are here now by *invitation only*. You are ONLY the same person in the same conditions that you were in yesterday because you choose to be. In any and every moment, you can grant yourself permission to make any change—in approach, thinking, behavior, addictions, tendencies, limiting beliefs, ANYTHING!

Achievers recognize that they have the right and responsibility to reinvent themselves, and there has never been a time in history in which we have had more flexibility to do just that. Today, we have more choices and fewer restrictions than in any previous time. Listen, in past times and especially in some countries, many of the choices that we now take for granted didn't exist. If, for instance, you were a young man raised in the 1700's, you would likely go to work at age fourteen or fifteen and start life as an apprentice for an established tradesman. This trade would become your career, your destiny, and there were very few circumstances where that could ever change. Same gig everyday for the rest of your working life. Now, in most developed countries, people change careers with ease. Another example of a situation where personal control over major life decisions was not available is the practice of arranged marriages—which, of course, is still the norm in some cultures today. Imagine having the decision about the person you will spend the rest of your life with, be completely out of your hands.

I bring up these two examples to provide you with some contrast so that you can compare these more structured lifestyles to your own life and opportunities now. For the most part, people now have the ability to choose their professions and their spouses and also have the luxury of controlling so many other aspects of their lives. However, what is fascinating is that even though we have the privilege of choosing our destiny, many of us lack the mental and emotional flexibility to capitalize on this world of opportunity. We, instead, remain in our comfort zone.

This comfort zone carries a very high price tag. Remember, comfort is not the same as happiness. Almost everyone talks about making changes to improve their lives. Why don't most people do it? One reason is that it takes an upfront commitment to be brave and to cross into the unknown. Perhaps, like them, you have come right up to the edge before, but then, right as you were about to take the next step, the one that took the most courage, the one that signaled commitment to a new, more exhilarating direction, you stepped back instead. If you want to break that cycle, keep reading. I have done it, and I will teach you how.

What prompts big changes?

It seems that for many, making a change in direction becomes an option only when extreme challenges show up and force the issue. There are countless stories of people who had finally had enough of what they were experiencing and, in that moment, pushed back against established norms and charted a new course. (The movie *Norma Rae* comes to mind.) But what does it mean when a person decides to reinvent themselves, not just because their back is against the wall, but proactively because they want more? That is the invitation here.

For risk to be not only tolerated but exciting, there needs to be an associated, offsetting reward. When you step across the line into what can feel like the unknown, you want to feel that you will find a greater version of *you* waiting there. You will expand in talent, wisdom, knowledge and skill—and new attributes suitable to the new challenges will be revealed. As you cross over that line to the path that calls you to your highest and best self, an increase in your self-awareness, confidence and authenticity will accompany you. All of these will stay hidden and dormant if, instead, you shrink back and settle.

"Surrender to what is.
Let go of what was.
Have faith in what will be."
—Sonia Ricotti

What does changing course require?

Thankfully, there are only a handful of things that it takes, and you have these all on board already. To step up and reinvent your future, you need:

1. Mental and emotional flexibility
2. To avoid focus on limitations
3. A commitment to stand strong and stay the course when things are difficult
4. To believe that the risk will be worth it
5. A core belief that life is not meant to be lived *out*, but rather, it is to be lived *in*
6. Willingness to stretch yourself

The only thing that matters is what you do from this point forward.

"Yesterday's over my shoulder, so I can't look backwards too long. There's too much to see waiting in front of me and I know I just can't go wrong."
—Jimmy Buffet

How to Recognize When It Is Time to Reboot and Make a Big Change

The voyage of self-development often calls you to discover and develop the greater person within you and then clear the way for that authentic greatness to be delivered through you and into the world. Along the road of life, you may see visions of what your life could—and maybe even should be. You might feel something inside nagging at you to make a move and it just won't shut up. The good news is, that nagging is looking out for you and the future you, and the fact that it won't shut up means that the time is near. Find that path, for it is in your expanding that new opportunities, skills, clarity, authenticity and joy arrive. Here are the ways that this inner guidance and external circumstances might be signaling you.

Signal # 1. The most common indicator that a big shift is needed is the answer to a most basic question: Is your life the way that you want it to be? No? Can you make it the way you want it to be on the path that you are on now? Yes? Great! Get busy fixing what needs to be fixed. But if you answered No, it's OK. You're not broken. You are just at a powerful crossroads. What are you being called to change?

Signal # 2. You find that you end up playing the same, dissatisfying role over and over in friendships and work relationships.

Signal # 3. You are discontented. It is not until a person becomes discontented with some part of their life that they will have the energy and stamina to move from what *is* to what *could be*. Successful individuals are blessed with the gift of an internal crisis or struggle that calls them to new levels of development. If you find yourself thinking, "Is this all there is?" the answer is *hell no!* Time to reinvent.

Signal # 4. You are *so* bored. Life feels dull. Day in and day out, you feel as though you are in a rut.

Signal # 5. You feel like a fraud. You are not on a mission and are routinely misaligned and out of synch with those in your personal and professional life.

> The perfect moment will never arrive,
> so don't waste time waiting for it.
> Listen to your gut, trust your instincts, make your move!

Here is one example of a person hearing the call to make a big change and successfully following that call. A good friend of mine had built a successful business and, while I never knew it, was also in a marriage that had run its course and was fading fast. She had an anchor client in another city that loved her and her work, and she believed she could grow that client relationship significantly if she were living near their corporate headquarters. She had a big choice to make. She was pretty sure that her husband would not make the move if she presented that option to him, and given the shakiness of the relationship, she wondered if going it alone and ending the relationship would actually be the best thing to do. While tons of fear washed over her, she presented the option of their moving to the new city to her husband. He responded with a resounding "No way," so she brought an end to the marriage and moved on solo to the new city.

As the lyrics in a popular song by The Fray explain, "Sometimes the right thing and the hard thing are the same thing."

It was really tough to take the bold step to end the marriage and the additional bold step of moving solo to a new town. Once there, she noticed that although there were times of loneliness, her primary emotion, day in and day out, had shifted from heaviness and sadness to joy and excitement about her future. As her energy shifted upward, so did her ability to be more present with others and her anchor client quickly responded by more than quadrupling the scope and revenue of her contract. She is now thriving and so much happier. Her awesome example supports the idea that having the strength to change your direction and reinvent yourself opens the door to abundance in many areas.

"If you're brave enough to say goodbye, life will reward you with a new hello."
—Paulo Coehlo

Reinvent and thrive—or remain stagnant and perish. For my friend, the signal that it might be time to do a reality check and maybe initiate a big change came both externally—through the increasing discontent with her marriage and increasing opportunity with her out-of-town anchor client—and internally, through a sense that these experiences were probably not coincidental, but rather a call to action.

First Three Steps to Take When You Are Ready to Make a Major Move

1. Give yourself permission...
   - to reboot and to have a "do-over"
   - to acknowledge and act on what you are feeling
   - to unhook from the need for approval from others

This is not a dress rehearsal—this is YOUR life! Bring back power to it!

Here's an example from my life, which has had some powerful reboots and do-over's: Throughout my career, I have enjoyed an increasingly intriguing set of business opportunities, which I attribute to my being able and willing to reinvent myself. Like some others, I first advanced through a series of corporate positions, then moved into starting my own business, then into several partnerships, then into sustaining my own business while going back into a full-time corporate position. Whew. Sounds like a lot of changes, but each has expanded my skills, abilities and perspective. I have accelerated my professional and personal development and knowledge tenfold when compared to what I would have experienced if I had stayed in a single job or field for twenty-five or thirty years. I found that it was in the times that I gave myself permission to deliberately reinvent that I was actually most energized and felt most alive.

2. Stop fighting for what has been.

This is the time to be disciplined about where you put your focus and energy. Depending on your personality, it will be either easy or difficult to shift your focus to where you are going, and not where you have been. If it is difficult for you and you find that you are holding on to where you have been, then you are working through a tug of war between what your gut is telling you to do and what you head is telling you to do. Recognizing when you are getting genuine guidance from your gut, versus just chatter, is a skill that can be learned. Learning to trust that genuine guidance is also a learnable skill. Making a big change in your life demands that you find a way to be fully aligned and clear. Having frequent periods of doubt will often derail your plans. There are few things more exhilarating than discovering that your gut, your inner guidance system, is on board and on track and there to accurately guide you. Remember that you are connected, protected, guided and loved and you are being called to a greater future through the clarity, vision and power of your inner guidance.

3. Get tactical.

Our analytical side often wants to see the plan. We can reduce the sense of uncertainty by spending time diving into the details and getting specific. This step is about linking the big picture vision for what we will create and experience on the other side of the big move with a detailed assessment of what we will need, when we will need it, and where we can get it. It is also about identifying what you want your role to be, what other skills you will require from others and the details and timeline for your transition. It is in the act of fleshing out the details and the action plan that your vision will become more and more clear, and that clarity creates the momentum you need and the excitement you want.

Successful Mindsets for Times of Big Change

One of the key components that separates deliberate evolution from just chasing the next shiny object is that first word—deliberate. Making a big move is not always simple and it is not always easy. It is a decision to step up into a more powerful expression of your skills and contribution. It is a commitment to play to your strengths and do what you can to trim your weaknesses. Deliberate evolution involves identifying what parts of you—your attributes, your passions, your talents, your strengths, you want to make sure you take with you into this new experience and which parts you will leave behind. The later list includes any attitudes, approaches, bad habits, inauthenticity, disempowering beliefs, and patterns and assumptions that cause undue stress, keep you playing small or just, in general, don't contribute to the level of effectiveness and happiness that you seek.

This is a change in mindset from shrinking back, to playing a bigger game, from wondering "Can I?" to owning "I will!" Not waiting anymore, but becoming what you can be.

"Somebody should tell us, right at the start of our lives, that we are dying. Then we might live life to the limit, every minute of every day. Do it! I say. Whatever you want to do, do it now!"
—Michael Landon

Let's look at two common derailers to those in the process of making big advances in their lives.

1. "FOMO"

FOMO is the fear of missing out. Missing out on opportunities that you might have had, had you chosen to go down another path. It is commonly experienced by those like you who seek to maximize their lives and therefore change course when so many others won't. "What if I had just stayed in my old job? By now my 401K and stock options would be vested." or "Maybe I should have stayed in that relationship, at least it was predictable." One challenge that we have is that no matter where we are, there is a part of us that is freaking out because we are fearful of what we might be missing out on with the other options that we had or have available. When in corporate jobs, we think, "Damn, I should get out of here and follow my passion, get my entrepreneur on." Then, when we make the move to do exactly that, to follow our passion, there are thoughts popping up like, "Wow, those company benefits sure were nice. Wish that I had those again."

So, what's the cure for FOMO? Don't dabble! Throw down, go all in. Recognize that reinvention involves wrestling with your own internal demons and the stories and fears they spin up. That's all they are, though—just stories. Is there something to them? Maybe. But FOMO can best be overcome by committing to go forward, not backward. Look, you are a smart and talented person. You will always have options available to you. There's no excuse for not pushing forward and pursuing what you want to create for yourself.

2. "Destiny DNA" and Learned Helplessness

Some believe that there is a single script for each of us to play out in this life. In much the same way that we have actual DNA in our bodies that govern many of our physical characteristics, some buy into the idea that our abilities and destinies are likewise predetermined and unchangeable. This is what I call the "Destiny DNA" myth. This leads to the belief that our habits, traits, patterns, ways of doing things and limitations are "just part of who we are" and can't be changed. What a cop-out that is! You are not a victim of any historical trait. Everything can be changed. There are no victims—there are only volunteers. And there are plenty of volunteers ready to dismiss their ability to create something better for themselves due to a preconceived notion of what they are able to accomplish.

Psychologist Martin Segelman refers to this as "Learned Helplessness." He has conducted extensive clinical research in the areas of depression and happiness and coined the phrase "Learned Helplessness" to describe a disempowering psychological state. He postulates that learned helplessness is a psychological response that conditions people who have encountered difficulty in a particular situation—to just give up—give up and accept an adverse outcome, even when the person has the power to change the situation. It's a powerful concept and a mindset that will kill momentum and halt progress.

Because we feel that we are not capable, we back that up by focusing on our shortcomings instead of our strengths. This, of course, means that if we are not careful, we can easily buy into thoughts that our shortcomings define us. We can begin to believe that we are destined for failure if we take the risk of stepping into the creation of our dreams because, according to Segelman's research, we come to believe that…

- Our challenges are unique and *personal*; that our challenges are reflections of us.
- Our challenges are *pervasive*, overlapping into all areas of our life.
- Our challenges are *permanent*—the way we have always been is how we will always be.

What is the opposite of this? An acknowledgement that our challenges are not personal, not pervasive, not permanent.

So, as author Richard Bach says, "Argue for your limitations, and, sure enough, they are yours." Focus on your ability to have and to be and do whatever you want—and that there are no limitations and no exceptions to that—and *that's* how it will be. If you find that your mindset is slipping as you attend to challenges, remember that the challenges are temporary, not personal, persuasive or permanent.

3. Examine and Change out Labels

We use labels to help us be more effective in our thinking and processing. Unfortunately, once we assign a label to something, like whether something is a strength or weakness for us or others, it can be difficult to change that label even after all evidence indicates that the label is no longer accurate. When talking about skills and aptitudes, labels have a shelf life and most will eventually expire and no longer be valid. After all, as human beings, we are always changing, always changed. Learning how to let go of how we labeled ourselves yesterday or one minute ago is part of the success plan.

I believe that many of our old beliefs are holding us back from progress, wasting our valuable time now and causing too much pain. Think of them in the following context and then ask yourself what rings true. My labels and beliefs might be...

- limiting my life choices
- limiting my joy
- weighing me down now
- stifling my sense of opportunity

Every improvement in life experience starts with a shift on the inside. When you learn to listen to that voice and embrace that shift, you will have the results that you seek.

REINVENTION ASSIGNMENT

Create a new set of labels that will support and empower you *now* and in each day, moving forward. Take out a clean sheet of paper and draw spaces for yourself to use to list your new, empowering labels. It should look somewhat like this (with as many lines as necessary). Fill up the page!

I am...

_____

_____

_____

_____

Here are some examples from my personal work and from clients that I have had the honor of working with.

I am vibrant, young in heart, mind and body
I am playful, intuitive and happy
I am grateful for everything that I have and will experience
I am strong, blessed and congruent
I am the master of my destiny and co-creator of my life
I am a magnifier of joy, potential and results
I am a leader, and I determine my results in advance
I am an endurance powerhouse
I am connected, protected, guided and loved
I never settle, period!

Your commitment to reinventing yourself is a bold statement to *yourself*, to those that know you, and to the spirit of life itself, that yours is a life that will be lived without limits and that your past, while so very valuable, has only taken place to create a solid platform from which you can make big and powerful changes.

"Your time is limited, so don't waste it living someone else's life. Don't be trapped by dogma, which is living with the results of other people's thinking. Don't let the noise of others' opinions drown out your own inner voice. And most important, have the courage to follow your heart and intuition. They somehow already know what you truly want to become."

—Steve Jobs

Reinvention is focused on moving forward in a way that will expand you and the quality of your life. It requires strength, faith, determination and the ability to trust and to let go. In the next chapter we will explore how to become masterful in the skill of trusting and letting go.

Chapter 6

Trust and Let Go

I n this book we have identified several ways to step up and make sure that you are in the driver's seat when it comes to taking control of your life. We have discussed being a strong Warrior, being Brave, Bold and Courageous, Mastering Resiliency and Reinventing Yourself when you need to, over and over, again and again. These are all important strengths and I hope that through reading and implementing what you have learned in this book, you have become more deliberate and more powerful as a committed individual and that you are more determined than ever to excel and, more importantly, to never settle again.

So why, after all of this, would we now address something as "soft-sounding" as trusting and letting go? On the surface, this seems to be almost the opposite of the action-focused topics that preceded this chapter. Listen, this is NOT a soft topic at all! You only get one lap around the track in this life. There is a clear beginning and a clear end. If you waste any time in the shadows not trusting enough in your own skills and not trusting in the support that exists outside of you,

you are wasting very precious time. Similarly, if you don't know how to recognize when it is time to let go of something, someone, some way of approaching things that doesn't fit anymore—or worse, if you do know that you need to let go, separate yourself and move on but you don't– you are not only wasting precious time but you are also slaughtering your energy. Creating the life, results and impact that you desire takes the combination of all of these skills.

We started back in the beginning of the book talking about the power of gratitude. We'll finish on the topics of trusting and letting go. Like bookends, these two concepts complement the high-action, "be-unstoppable" concepts discussed in the chapters in between. These are foundational. Perhaps most importantly, anchoring to a foundation of gratefulness and knowing when to trust, to loosen your grip, to let go, is critical to the ability to live a life of more ease and less stress, of more grace and less wear and tear, and (*here's the kicker*)… better results and more success.

We will begin this chapter by looking at Trust and follow that with its close partner, Letting Go. This progression makes sense, as it also takes a measure of trust in order to be willing to release and let go.

Here are the four ways that increasing your level of trust will pay off for you:

1. Trust paves the way for intelligent risk-taking.
2. Trusting is good for business.
3. Trust combats worry.
4. Trust sharpens your instincts and enhances your intuition.

The Role of Trust in Risk-taking

Risks create rewards. Trust creates the confidence needed to take intelligent risks. It takes trust before you can access the courage to let go of solid footing and leap into the unknown in the hope that you will be OK. It works something like this: Imagine the amount of trust it takes to be standing on the top of a cliff about to rappel for the first time. Rappelling involves being connected to a rope that is anchored to something at the top, then, using the rope, lowering yourself off the cliff such that your body is now perpendicular to the vertical wall of the cliff and parallel to the ground that's way below you. Standing on flat ground at the top of the cliff, harness on, rope connected to the rappel gear around your waist—that is the time to lean back and walk off the cliff. This is one of those times when every cell in your body is saying, "Wait! You're going to do WHAT?" As you let a little more rope slide through your fingers and through the rappel gear, a threshold moment occurs and in order for you avoid smashing yourself into the cliff wall, you must trust and let go even more in order to maintain your horizontal orientation, ensuring that it is your feet, not your head bouncing off the rock face.

It takes trust before we can let go of other things in life also—trust that you don't have to know what is around every curve, trust that you can stretch yourself beyond what is known and comfortable. Progress occurs when we are able to shift to deeper levels of trust.

Wouldn't it be awesome if we knew for sure that we were guaranteed to be successful in any endeavor we wanted to undertake? But, hey, that is not how it works. Those guarantees aren't there. It is only through forward movement into the unknown, movement based on trust, that we find the strength, resourcefulness and connectedness to create what we desire. Creating what we want in our lives requires that we be willing to walk out through a door and down a path that we can't yet fully see and don't yet fully know.

Major payoff: Taking risks keeps you young!

Here is a real world example of someone using these exact tools that you are learning—and making what many would consider an extreme decision. A client, Madeline, is an exceptionally talented marketing consultant who, like many, wasn't in love with her career path. She really enjoyed the nuts and bolts of marketing, especially when she was in a position to apply her creative abilities, but she was struggling with the office politics and the restrictions placed on her by managers. She had recently changed agencies in the hopes that a new work environment and culture would reignite her passion. The change didn't make anything better.

As we talked, she shared with me that her brother had recently reached out to her, completely out of the blue, without knowing anything about her present career challenges, and proposed that she fly down to meet him in Australia—and then head out with him on a three-month trip through several countries in Asia. Wow! What great fun that would be! She had been pondering this idea and had become frustrated trying to come up with the "right" answer. She asked me for perspective and advice. The trip sounded amazing and she knew that that time with her brother would build on the already strong bond that they had. At the same time, she said, "I don't have the money for something like this."

I told her the story of the gentleman from India whom I had met in the airport. As you will recall, his core message was that our best answers come from our hearts, not from our heads. Madeline and I went through a guided meditation specifically designed to strengthen her connection to her heart and intuition. As we concluded, she committed to continue focusing her attention on the messages from her heart. She would call me when she had arrived at the decision.

Three days later I heard back from her. She had booked the flight, given her employer notice, and resigned from her job. She was on a plane to Australia three weeks later. Madeline decided to take a risk and trust the guidance from her heart. She let go of the need to always play it safe. She mentioned that the story of the gentleman from India and his nudge to listen to her heart instead of her head gave her the confidence to take the risk.

When Madeline came back to the United States, she called to tell me that going on that trip was a life-changing experience and the best decision she had ever made. What had initially felt very risky, ended up creating clarity for her. While away she realized that what was missing in her previous jobs was missing for a reason. She realized that she was being called to open her own marketing agency, become her own boss, and create a company culture that she and her team thrived in. She reconnected to her passion. The risk paid off for her.

In what area have you been avoiding taking a risk that, once taken, could change your life forever?

Trusting Is Good Business!

The act of trusting actually makes you smarter. When we come from a place of trust, we are more confident than when we are in fear and doubt. Let me give you an example of how trust can win the day in business situations. Recently, I was talking to John, who is building a very cool language-learning business in New York City (www.cityspeakeasy.com). He and his partners had worked hard to build the business. Their product was solid and, as their students completed courses, news of the company was spreading. Like many start-up entrepreneurs, they were self-funded and burning cash, though. Their biggest challenge was getting the revenue up fast enough.

The success of each semester was critical. Three weeks away from the start of their next semester, enrollment was far below where they needed it to be, and the partners, while trying to stay positive, were freaking out. "Here's the deal," I said to him, "you can never attract what you want (in this case more students) from a place of desperation, fear and doubt. When we are desperate and approach things as if our backs are against the wall, two things happen: First, other people, including clients and prospects, pick up on that desperate vibe and that does not build the kind of compelling confidence needed for them to get out their credit cards. Anyone who has spent any time in sales knows that when you need to close the deal on the table to make your quota, and maybe even to keep your job, the hardest thing to do is keep that desperation hidden—and those deals become tough to land. And the opposite is true. When you are well above quota and completely out of the danger zone, opportunities seem to arrive more easily and sales close with relatively far less effort. Secondly, when we are desperate, we often move into control mode, believing that we need to control everything that we can in order for things to work out."

Here is the problem. This sense of needing to control, when combined with desperation, triggers the release of a hormone called cortisol. Cortisol is released as a response to stress. It moves us out of composure and Big Picture clarity and into survival, fight-or-flight mode. This is awesome if we fall over the fence at the zoo and are faced with hungry tigers moving toward us. Strategic thinking and a focus on our long-term goals will mean very little in that situation. Thankfully, though, we are rarely faced with such life or death situations these days.

Our bodies still release cortisol in response to stress, however, and the effect is that we lose our mental edge. When immersed in stress, we make poorer decisions. When we feel desperate, the channels to our creativity and best answers close down.

You can quickly identify those times when stress and desperation have taken over. Stress takes up a tremendous amount of mental energy, drains us emotionally, and shuts down our connection to our wisdom and fortitude. In other words, when we are desperate and our ego throws us into control mode, we quickly become drained of our intellectual power and, thus, less effective. Worse, when we are in control mode, focus can slip up and move completely into our heads as we desperately search for answers in our "figure-it-all-out" brain. We lose that connection to the guidance and wisdom that we have highlighted frequently in this book that comes from our hearts. We become so wrapped up in trying to think through it and figure out "the" answer ourselves that we pinch off the connection to that inner wisdom that is always present, sitting there in standby mode, waiting to get involved and intervene on our behalf.

When you find yourself stressed out and really needing your ship to come in, remember that the energy associated with that desperation will likely push away what you most want and need. Instead, you can deliberately choose to come from a stance of relaxed confidence. It sounds simple—maybe too simple, but instead of moving toward control, try stepping back and trusting. Find your best ways to remain calm and envision the offer coming in, the sale getting done, the customer saying "Yes." Desperation doesn't sell. Relaxed confidence sells.

Trust More or Keep Worrying? Your choice.

Worry functionally ensures that you will not find the best answers, the ones that will get you back on track and attracting the results, lifestyle and wealth that you seek and deserve. Worry and its corollary, fear, through their very nature, shift our focus to what you DO NOT want to happen.

Fear will make you question whether or not you should act on what's in your heart. Aren't you tired of feeling the heaviness that fear and worry bring? Were we really meant to have limited experiences of life just because of what *might* happen? I don't believe so.

I'm offering you an opportunity to re-think, and maybe right-size the role of fear and worry in your life and replace them with higher levels of trust and confidence.

Here are a few of my favorite thoughts about worry:

- Worry is the misuse of imagination.
- Worry is praying for what you *don't* want.
- Worry is the price you pay in advance for most of the things that never happen in your life.

What stories are you blowing up in your head right now? Ask yourself how likely it is that these scary stories are anything but illusions. Are any of these things you fear likely to happen? Fears and worries that are closely and honestly examined tend to fade away. Look at fear as a chance to check in on the level of your commitment. Fear and worry are nothing more than a personal assignment to learn and grow.

"I am an old man and have known a great many troubles, but most of them never happened."
—**Mark Twain**

Trust Your Instincts. Trust Your Intuition—
They Are Real Assets

The key to power is not always might. Sometimes it takes the most strength to follow your instincts and listen to your intuition. When we were younger, that was an easy and natural thing to do. But over the years, that is a talent that can fade. Your instincts and intuition have always been with you, but if you have not nurtured them and developed a strong connection to them, they have likely atrophied, and it will take some time for you and your instincts and intuition to get reacquainted. In any moment, you can only either doubt your "gut" feeling and dismiss it as illogical or acknowledge it and listen more closely to it. One way or the other—you are either dialing the volume down or up on these two critical guides.

It can feel uncomfortable to listen for the subtle voice of this internal guidance, especially when your "figure-it-out" mind is yelling as loudly as it can to divert your attention and insist that it has the right answer for you. But it's when we're in that vulnerable place, when we trust and allow the voice of our internal guidance to be heard, that our most impactful breakthroughs occur.

Vulnerable—*yikes!* That's a terrifying word for many people. If the idea of being vulnerable strikes fear into your heart, I can understand—particularly since in many cultures men, especially, are trained from an early age to be strong, suck it up and not show any signs of weakness. Vulnerability is actually a powerful strength. Here's why embracing vulnerability delivers strong advantages.

It is only by accepting your vulnerability that you can access your true *invulnerability.* You might well ask, "How can opening up and becoming vulnerable lead to strength? Doesn't vulnerability equate to weakness? That is the illusion. Vulnerability is the outward expression of an internal release into trust. It is a form of deliberate surrender. It requires trust. And when you have a high enough level of trust, you can begin to let go.

To initiate a breakthrough you might be used to applying your drive, might and tenacity in an effort to shatter limitations and overcome obstacles. Interestingly, though, many of the most significant breakthroughs occur when we unhook from powering through and finally release into vulnerability and intuition.

Override your conditioning. Trust your instincts and trust your intuition.

Letting Go

When you are frustrated, freaked out, tired and repeating bad habits over and over—stop and step back for a minute and ask, "Wait a second, is there something here that I need to let go of?" More than anything external, we are most often the force slowing down our progress and momentum. To know what to let go of and when to let go is the second most important skill to have. *(We'll talk about the most important one soon.)* The most successful business owners and managers know to hire slowly and fire quickly. Another way of saying it is, "Be willing to let go of what is no longer a fit… and do it fast."

Do you remember the storybook character Curious George? He was a monkey who found himself in a big city and seemed to find a way to get into mischief on a regular basis. One particular day he saw a man selling helium balloons on the street corner. George just couldn't resist, and while the man was not paying attention, he reached over and grabbed the entire bundle. Turned out, there was more lift with those balloons than there was weight on that monkey, and George found himself rising into the air. If he'd let go right then, he would have only dropped a few feet and been safe. But George didn't let go and was now high up in the air. Letting go at that point would mean a long fall to the hard pavement below.

He didn't let go fast enough. Now he was paying the price.

There is a right time to let go. Holding on too tight for too long will almost always create new and bigger problems for us, just like it did for George. If you feel stuck, check in to see if it is time to let go of something.

There are times in everyone's life when we have held onto something too long, something that was no longer right for us—a job, a career, a relationship, a friendship, an expectation, a tired old limiting belief. Letting go is not always easy—and it's certainly not always convenient, but that doesn't make it any less urgent or real if we are to have the success and fulfillment that we desire. Even more important, though, is actually having the strength to let go of that which needs to be released. The awareness of a need to let go of something is important, but taking action and actually releasing and moving on is critical.

Some people and some experiences are in our lives for a reason, some for a season, and some for a lifetime. Recognizing when something or someone may not be destined to be in your life forever is the starting point. Success often requires letting go of what used to work. It's OK. You and the people around you are constantly evolving. You are simply not the same person today that you were when you made the decisions that landed you where you find yourself now. And neither are they. It's OK.

> "In the end, only three things matter: How much you loved, how gently you lived, and how gracefully you let go of things not meant for you."
> —Buddha

Check in with yourself. Are there relationships or habits or patterns that used to energize you, but that now just feel heavy?

Not making needed changes will eventually wear you down. It's like getting up every morning and loading up a backpack with several five-pound rocks, then putting that heavy pack on and carrying it around all day. Then, once you're back home, you continue to carry the full pack until you finally crash and roll into bed. The next morning, instead of saying, "Wow, I'm so glad I don't have to carry those rocks around anymore," you load up and start all over again. Seems like a pretty insane thing to do, right?

This is exactly what we do when we know that something is no longer a fit, but we don't do anything about it. Stop! Take off the pack. Unload it once and for all.

SOME OTHER THINGS TO LET GO OF...

Let Go of Tribal Thinking

In Richard Bach's book, *Illusions* (one of my favorite books ever), he describes a colony of insects that live under the water in a brook. While all the others grasp tightly to reeds and blades of grass as they always have—and as their ancestors always did—one of the members of the insect colony decided one day to simply let go of the reed and enter the flow of the brook just to see where it took him and what that experience would be like. He finds that the current that the others had warned would surely smash him against the rocks and kill him, instead, lifted him up high and carried him safely on a voyage that allowed him to see the great expanse of the brook—and into an even more amazing river.

Instead of listening to the traditional thinking of his tribe, he listened to his heart, trusted in himself, and let go.

The doors of life open when leaned against with confidence. Life opens up for those who decide to let go of the norms and reach out for more. Imagine for a moment that there is a positive conspiracy in place. It is a conspiracy always at the ready to support you, to show you safe passage through the woods—a positive conspiracy waiting for you to let go of your need for certainty so that you can experience more.

Let Go of Comparison and Control

In my work with individuals and teams, the following are routinely the most difficult things to release—and also the most freeing and the most rewarding for people once the release is made. Power and strength are restored when we...

- let go of the need to make others wrong.
- let go of the need to be right.
- let go of our facades.

- stop keeping score.
- stop comparing ourselves to others.
- let go of the need for significance.
- learn how to ask for what we want.
- say what we need to say.

And when we finally...

- recapture the energy we spend trying to change other people.
- stop ruminating about what someone else should or should not be doing.
- let the chips fall where they may and know that we will be OK.
- unhook from the need for the good opinion of other people.

Reread the list again. How many of these are challenges for you?" Is now the time to change an old habit or two so that you can recapture energy and be more congruent and aligned with your values?

"What others think of me is none of my business."
—Anonymous

Let Go of Thinking that You Have the Right Answers for Other People

Sometimes we overinflate our role. A few years ago, I made a discovery that certainly didn't sit well with me. Unintentionally, through my actions and words, I was perceived as being pretty judgmental, especially by some of my family members. This came with a high cost to some of my relationships. Without being aware of it, a few of the people closest to me had come to feel that I was disappointed and frustrated with them. I didn't feel disappointed or frustrated, but when I reflected on this a bit more, I could understand how they might have felt that way. I could see how my personal approach to life, which is basically about maximizing everything and every minute and every day, could get pretty annoying if that was not their core approach to life, too. I realized that while my clients often hired me to push them, knock them out of their comfort zone, and hold them accountable for what they committed to accomplish, that is not what my family wanted AT ALL.

Lesson learned the hard way. As a coach I needed to keep my coaching skills at the office and apply them to help those who sought me out. I came to realize that those who were not asking me to be their coach REALLY didn't want that from me. Makes perfect sense to me now.

I took some time to digest this feedback and made a decision that I had to change my ways. I choose to consciously release my family members to live the lives, have the experiences, accomplishments, and setbacks that only they know they are here to experience. Releasing and letting go of my thought that I should monitor their progress or success, or that I had the right answers for them, was simply right-sizing my role. Letting go of this was not lowering my standards, but rather, returning to the place that I should have been all along.

Here's the thing: It's important to let go of the need to be such an integral force in the lives of other people—that is not your role. Let go of the need to try to change any other person. We are each on our own journey. Let's face it, I don't always know what lessons I am here to learn. How could I possibly know what lessons someone else is here to learn?

Working to change another person is the single biggest waste of time—period! Fully release them to have their experiences and learn their unique lessons without having to carry the burden of your judgment with them.

Where can you "right-size" your role?

Let Go of the 24 Hour "Do" Fest

When was the last time you slowed down enough to see if all that you were doing was actually getting you what you wanted? If you can swing it, schedule a personal retreat. Your "personal retreat" is really just a dedicated time away from your daily tasks and a deliberate break in your routine. This is a chance to pull your raft out of the rapids and into the still backwaters.

"When people wish to see their reflections, they do not look into running water, they look into still water. Only that which is still can hold other things still."
—Chuang Tsu

Sometimes we have to slow down in order to speed up. Given the fast pace of our lives these days, many people struggle with the idea of taking time to be away. Becoming still is a talent that most haven't mastered, and yet it is only in the stillness that we can get reacquainted with ourselves. As we allow the tight weave to relax and loosen, the ideas and answers that we are looking for have a chance to appear.

Retreat is an attitude, not a destination. If you can get away to a beach or the mountains or a place that you enjoy, that's great. But realize that you can also accomplish this by scheduling an afternoon spent at a coffee shop or in a park.

During your retreat spend some time reflecting on:

1. What am I most happy with in my life?
2. What is working well?
3. What needs my attention now?
4. During what activities do I feel most real and authentic?
5. What do I want the next two years of my life to represent?
6. What are my top goals for the next year?
7. What do I need to let go of to achieve those goals?
8. How am I being called to grow?

Often times you can find yourself only by losing yourself. "...when you lose yourself, you find the key to Paradise."
—Zac Brown, *Knee Deep*

Let Go of the Need to Control It All

When a NASCAR or Formula One driver is in an accident on the race track and the car begins to spin, the driver is trained to let go of the steering wheel. It has been proven that trying to control a car in that situation will only make things worse. In a similar way, there are times when our desire to control things definitely makes things worse.

We have on our "tool belts" that contain whatever we need to fix most challenges or problems. And no one tool is the right tool for every situation. If your normal response is to try to control things, try out the other tools on your belt, such as the tool of releasing and letting go. We are wise to know when to apply control and force and when the right move is to release and take our hands off the wheel.

But how will you know when? Here is a tool that you can use:

Three-Question Reality Check
1.   What can you actually influence?
2.   What can you control?
3.   What do you have neither influence nor control over?

In my experience, the list of things that can be *influenced* is large. The list of those that can be *controlled* is small. There is a right time to steer and a right time to let go of the wheel.

Sometimes it's OK to not know, to just let go and let the boat drift a bit. When you do, the wind may just come up and take you in a great new direction.

Let Go of the Leash

Ask yourself where you are following, when you should be leading. Are you being pulled through life or are you in charge?

Gliders are just like regular planes except they have no motor. A glider relies on a motorized plane to take it up to altitude. It is a very bumpy, uncomfortable ride while under tow. At the exact right moment, the glider pilot pulls a handle which releases the tether that connects it to the pull plane and a complete separation occurs. It is only in that release that the experience of genuine smooth, peaceful and exhilarating flight takes place.

Too often in the relatively short span of human life, people forget to let go and release. Being pulled through life by being a workaholic, accepting labels and other people's rules for how we need to be and being stressed out all the time is missing the point of life. What is pulling you that you can let go of so that you can finally experience your own true flight—so that you can experience some freedom and some blue sky?

Letting Go of the Idea that Things Need to Be Difficult to Be Valuable

Sometimes the harder we try, the harder it is. Applying intensity, dedication and energy to what we want to create is important, but, like most things, there is a point of diminishing returns. Do you really need to try SO hard to get or build what you want—like business results? What about backing out of the struggle from time to time, leaving some room for other forces to step in on your behalf?

When we are so committed to drive-drive-drive, we may be closing the door on all of the serendipitous and magical forces that could bring us more than we ever imagined. Knowing when to take your foot off the gas pedal is as important as knowing when to "floor it."

EXERCISE
Letting Go of the Need to Believe that It Has to Be Difficult

Consider the following questions:

- Would it actually be alright with me if my life became easier?
- What if this *could* be a lot easier than I am making it?
- How can I have this situation be easier?
- What is the best and fastest way to advance this plan?
- What's the easiest and most fun way to make this happen?
- Who would I be if I let go of the need to struggle?
- What am I holding onto too tightly?

Although hard work and persistence can lead to accomplishment, breakthroughs in results and fulfillment often occur from letting go— especially letting go of an old stale set of rules.

Letting Go of Needing to Always Lead the Charge

When you watch a bicycle race like the Tour de France, one thing you'll see for sure is something called "drafting." There are times when the right move for a competitor is to power through, break out ahead of the pack, and take the lead. There are other times when the wiser strategy is to slip back behind another biker and draft, staying close enough to allow the other rider to battle the headwind for you. Naturally, this second strategy allows you to go farther faster, while expending significantly less energy—and all the while, you're looking for the right time to make your move

Getting from Point A to Point B in cycling, as in business and in life, does not take the same amount of energy for everyone. Some try to gut it out and stay out in front without the benefit of splitting the load and drafting. But sometimes the more intelligent, nuanced approach is to let go of the lead position and allow other forces—whatever they may be—to cover for you and lighten the load a bit.

ONE LAST THOUGHT ON RELEASING AND LETTING GO...

It may seem counterintuitive, but whatever you really want, *unhook yourself from the need to have that!* What? Yep, if you want success, let go of the need for success. If you want love, let go of the need for love. If you want happiness, let go of the need for happiness. If you want respect, let go of the need for respect. If you want recognition, let go of the need for recognition.

When we are caught up in the need for something, strangely, that "need energy" will actually push away what we want. Release the sense of need and create room for what you want to show up on its own.

"We hold on to what we hold on to and let go of what we choose to let go of. We hold onto patterns and weaknesses for a reason— this gives us our excuses not to shine."
—Maryanne Williamson

When I was a novice speaker and trainer, I was invited to a company to provide a two-day training session. By midmorning of the first day, I began to feel somewhat unappreciated and undervalued (hello Ego!). Naturally, this was disturbing to me, and dealing with this moved me more and more into my head. Soon, I realized what was happening and why I was feeling that way. I had allowed myself to make this training about me, about whether or not I was doing a good job and about whether or not the participants were impressed with my material and delivery. This is not the key to success for a trainer—or anyone else!

As soon as you let it become about *you*, you have lost your focus on what is actually important, which, in this case, was the participants and whether or not they were getting what they needed to become better and more effective leaders. Fortunately, in this situation, I was able to mentally step back and deliberately release myself from the triggers that created my oversized need for appreciation and recognition. When I took a few minutes to step away and rebalance my emotional portfolio, I was able to let go of those needs.

Surprisingly to me at the time, as I re-engaged with a focus, not on me and what I was getting or not getting, but on the experience of the participants, was that I wound up connecting more powerfully and delivering a more impactful experience—and I ended up receiving all of the recognition, acknowledgement and positive feedback that I was seeking in the first place.

It's the most beautiful irony and the truest form of self-exploration and self-knowledge to discover that in the letting go of the need to be recognized or lauded, we release the very fear that blocks us from receiving what we want. When we allow ourselves to be authentic and vulnerable and release from the energy that surrounds need, the floodgates open for us to receive what we most desire.

Whatever you want, say "YES" to it and let it come to you. The only thing that may be standing between you and whatever you want is YOU!

Warriors are not only brave, bold and courageous, not only masterful in their ability to bounce back up, to get back in and fight, not only decisive when it is time to reinvent themselves and willing to make needed changes quickly but Warriors also walk with grace from the foundation of gratefulness. Warriors know that trusting is not making them more vulnerable; rather, it is the key to being even *more* powerful and invulnerable. They know when and how to let go of things, people, and approaches that once fit, but do not anymore.

Warriors live life on *their* terms committed to massive action, massive contribution and massive impact. You are a Warrior! Lead your life with strength and grace.

Final Thoughts

So, there you have it. Having enjoyed the phenomenal privilege of mentoring many people who were already near the top of their game—and many who were building up to their greatness, I have had the opportunity to see how people from all backgrounds have constructed lives of great success. I have not only witnessed the perseverance of those who have boot-strapped and brought about their own success through sheer will and determination—but I have also seen others who came from privileged backgrounds of great financial, emotional and educational support suffer on the downward spiral of ineffectiveness, depression and self-destruction.

It was in my seeking to identify what differentiates people who enjoy lives of joy and success from those who seem consistently frustrated and stuck that led me to dig in and pinpoint the behaviors, actions and attitudes that make the difference. It became clear to me that those living in a state of joy and success lived from a foundation of gratefulness. They took risks, were authentic and didn't focus on fitting in. They had the determination and tenacity of a warrior. They took setbacks in stride and figured out how to bounce back with amazing speed. They were willing to change course when needed and to reinvent their vision of themselves and what was possible. And they learned to trust in themselves, their intuition, and to let go of what no longer fit in their vision of their future.

While I don't know where you find yourself in your life right now or where you see your opportunities and challenges, what I do know is that you've got what it takes to build the life, career and business that you desire. The opportunities in front of you will help you reach, stretch and grow. The challenges will teach you important lessons, and each holds a gift for you that you will one day appreciate. Everything about what's happening with you, and for you, is in your life for a reason. I invite you to embrace the events and circumstances of each day as true blessings, for it is both the great accomplishments and the great challenges that sculpt us into the unstoppable people that we are.

You are at yet another critical point of decision. You, and only you, will make the choice to hold to your comfort zone and status quo or to leap forward and leave thoughts of impossible behind. What you *can* accomplish is unlimited. What you *will* accomplish is up to you.

I believe in you and I know that if you want it…

You've Got This!

About the Author

Will Matthews is a Board Certified Executive Coach and is CEO of Matthews Performance Group, a professional development and training company. Since 2003, he has used his passion for helping people create huge success to coach and train thousands of executives and professionals in organizations ranging from Fortune 100 companies to early stage start-ups. He has personally developed high performing sales and marketing teams and advanced the skills of operations teams from "the shop floor to the C-Suite" through his coaching, workshops and seminars. Will is an Expert Resource Speaker for Vistage International, a global CEO and Key Executive Leadership Development Forum, and hosted his radio show "Business and Beyond with Will Matthews, Your Personal Connection for Success!" Will lives in Denver, Colorado, is the father to four amazing people and is an Ironman Triathlon competitor.

To learn more about additional personal and professional development programs available from Matthews Performance Group please contact us at:

Phone: 720-300-6310

Email: info@mpgcoaching.com

Website: www.mpgcoaching.com

A free eBook edition is available with the purchase of this book.

To claim your free eBook edition:

1. Download the Shelfie app.
2. Write your name in upper case in the box.
3. Use the Shelfie app to submit a photo.
4. Download your eBook to any device.

Shelfie

A free eBook edition is available
with the purchase of this print book.

CLEARLY PRINT YOUR NAME ABOVE IN UPPER CASE

Instructions to claim your free eBook edition:
1. Download the Shelfie app for Android or iOS
2. Write your name in **UPPER CASE** above
3. Use the Shelfie app to submit a photo
4. Download your eBook to any device

Print & Digital Together Forever.

Snap a photo

Free eBook

Read anywhere

The Morgan James Speakers Group

www.TheMorganJamesSpeakersGroup.com

We connect Morgan James published authors with live and online events and audiences whom will benefit from their expertise.

CPSIA information can be obtained
at www.ICGtesting.com
Printed in the USA
LVOW08s2302160217
524502LV00003BA/769/P